Five Steps and a Jump!

Break Free and Embrace the Adventure God has Planned for You

Five Steps and a Jump!

Break Free and Embrace the Adventure God Has Planned for You

Bob Black

reify press
Portland, Oregon

Acknowledgments

Where else can I begin than to thank God for getting my attention and drawing me to him. Will I ever know the countless people you used in his grand scheme? What greater love is there than this? Now to be used by you to advance your kingdom; I remain in awe.

I read this morning Proverbs 18:22: "The man who finds a wife finds a treasure, and he receives favor from the Lord." Sue, you are my treasure. What a blessing you have been, supporting me in my journey. Clearly, you are one that God used to reach me. I could never have known God so well had it not been for your support, companionship and faith. You have fully supported me in making S Curve Jumps and now, once again you are right here with me. What better treasure could I have found? I love you, Sue!

Then I must call out my "Team," who provide such deep caring support and godly advice. Who would go to battle without the advice of trusted counsel? Brad, always leading by example, pushing me deeper in my faith and spiritual disciplines. You inspire courage. A true friend who would do anything for me. I owe so much to you for leading me to know Christ as an intimate. You are my brother.

Brent, such an endless source of encouragement who has been with me, side by side as a coach. I cannot tell you, my friend, how inspirational you are to me. You are the definition of positivity.

Jeff, you share your gifts of wisdom and strategic thinking so freely with me. You have helped me think through things, broaden my perspective and helped me dig deeper into my thoughts. Truly an advisor and vital part of my life.

How cool it has been to work with my son, Bobby, himself an author, who tapped into years of making comics to create the graphic illustrations in this book. Somehow, you make stick figures come to life and I find that I relate to them in some strange but innocent way. I love you Bobby! And thank you, Phil Disney of Clarity Design Studio, for cleverly incorporating them into the cover and interior graphics.

Anna, my daughter, is always a great source of positive encouragement for me. You have a way of just saying, "Why not go for it?!" So, here I am! I love you, Anna!

How could all of this come together without the clarifying deep thinking of Roger Shipman of Reify Press? You transformed my concepts into something real and tangible, I pray now a blessing for many. What an inspiration to see you Jump your S Curves in the midst of all of this work!

Preface

The wild ride I'm on began almost 20 years ago. I don't quite remember when I became a follower of Jesus Christ, but I can sure tell you what has happened since. Through a series of changes, he has transformed my life, opening my eyes to see and experience things I never could have dreamed of. Life was pretty good back then. I wasn't really looking for an adventure. Perhaps it found me. In any case, it has been incredibly freeing and brought a wonderful sense of fulfillment to my life. And it all started by taking a seemingly small step toward God.

Not long after becoming a follower, my wife and I sensed that something in our lives needed to change. But what? And why? We felt stuck, out of place.

Ever felt like this?

But with that one small step, soon things began to move, literally. Just a few weeks later, it was "suggested" I move across the country. A huge out-of-the-box life change. Coincidence? We grew closer to God in the process.

A few years later, I again was feeling off-kilter—trapped, held hostage by my work, which, after almost 20 years, had become dry, frustrating, and unfulfilling. I thought, "There has to be more to life than this!" What could I do? My family depended on my income; how could I even think of making a change? Fear gripped me.

Many I saw near me also appeared to be trapped. What was holding us hostage? Were they afraid like I? Soon, it seemed, I noticed people everywhere who were stuck, not fully living, each of us in a prison of unhappy work, many at things they were unsuited to do. It made no sense. I asked, "What are we doing? Are we all crazy?" These thoughts troubled me—something needed to change. As I drew near to God, he stirred me to start down a path that ultimately led me to make a major career change. Yikes! Scary . . . yet freeing and fulfilling at the same time! And in the process, I grew closer than ever to God.

Another few years passed. Again, one small step led to more significant life changes and I drew closer yet to God. Now he's led me to write this book, a challenge that seems way beyond me. But who's to say what God might do? All along, I have simply followed Proverbs 16:33 (a favorite): "You can roll the dice, but the Lord determines how they fall." I decided to be willing, and my life has not stopped moving; I have appreciated an increasing sense of freedom and fulfillment. There *is* more to life than this! I haven't looked back.

I said to myself, "I need to help those who are imprisoned like I had been to break free . . . and the sooner the better!" Life is too short to spend it as a captive.

While combing through all the changes I'd been through, it hit me that the key that freed me from being trapped each time fit a pattern I knew well. I want to share it with you.

My goal in writing this book is to provide you with new language and a framework to help you make sense of where you are at every point along your journey. Do you feel trapped? How can you break free, unlocking yourself from what seems inevitable captivity? God always provides a way out. But how do you find it? I will coach you through a Five-Step Process, also known as the Mission Curve Process, that will lead you to find your path of freedom where you can live the incredibly fulfilling life you were meant to live. You will answer some of life's biggest questions: "Why am I here, now?" and "What am I supposed to do with my life?" and the one that pops into my head all the time: "Isn't there more to life than this?"

One outcome will be to find a sense of purpose by developing a transformational Life Mission. When I rearranged my life around a mission, I found meaning and clear direction for my adventure. Life-altering decisions led to incredible experiences of God in action. My life began to align with God's plan for me. So powerful and eye-opening! As I moved toward accomplishing my mission, a vision formed of what lay ahead; I could not have seen it were I not already moving forward. God opened my eyes to see and to write out the big picture of how the future might look:

"I see a growing community of people of all ages that have been freed to live passionate and ever-growing lives. They continue to innovate their lives, growing deeply intimate with God, becoming one in purpose with him. They are gaining a greater and greater understanding of who God made them to be; accepting God's challenge to fully use their spiritual gifts as they pursue his purpose for their lives. They are willing to take the path of adventure at the cost of being comfortable as they courageously pursue their unique Life Mission. They share their testimonies to encourage and support each other's journey. As they lean forward and embrace their freedom, they discover that they are living truly fulfilling lives, way beyond their wildest expectations."

My prayer is that you will join this community by venturing down your own path of adventure, experiencing God intimately as you pursue his unique purpose for you, finding freedom and fulfillment along the way. Who's to say where God may take you on your adventure? Aren't you curious? It starts when you take that first small step closer to God, igniting the process of transformation through an ever-deepening intimate relationship with the one who made you. Moving forward will also help me fulfill the mission that God has asked me to pursue: "Unlocking lives, guiding futures." It's time to get started on the ride of your life. Let me show you the way.

Table of Contents

Introduction

God has hidden deep, unspoken desires within us and our souls cry out for freedom and meaning, to be our true selves, to make a difference, for things we enjoy and are passionate about. Yet everything works against this. The world traps and imprisons us. We ache for intimacy, to be known and loved unconditionally for who we are. We want to be honest yet loved. In our quest, we turn over every stone, yet come up short. Eventually we resolve to fall into line with everyone else to endure our sentence here on earth. Ugh...

I remember this exact place many years ago now. After nearly twenty years in the medical device industry I had come to a fork in the road. Something just wasn't right. Despite a career of success and advancement, I was tired and bored. My boss said, "Same old problems, just different characters." I was slogging through, just to do it all over the next day. Don't get me wrong; it was good work, and I was reasonably proficient. Grateful, I made a comfortable living. Yet I wondered, "Can I see doing this for the rest of my life?" I couldn't shake the gnawing question: "Isn't there more to life than this?" I had built my life around my career. I had young kids to support, college costs in the future, retirement to save for. How could I be such a fool as to give up a good, secure job? Fear had me trapped, locked in. What should I do?!

Are you there right now? Trust me, you are not alone. All of us find ourselves in this situation many times in our lives. I can assure you, there is hope for you. I shudder at the thought that I could still be stuck where I was. There is a path to freedom and fulfillment, to satisfy our deepest longings for intimacy. I am so glad I chose the path of adventure.

If we take a small step to engage God, he brings us into his adventure and directs us to the fulfillment of our desire for a vibrant, meaningful life in intimate relationship with him. I learned this after reflecting on significant life transitions over the past 25 years. God has opened my eyes to see that we follow the natural pattern of the S curve, a well-known concept in the business world that you may find familiar as we go forward. Incredibly, applying these concepts to my work and spiritual lives has opened me up to an amazing adventure beyond my wildest expectations. Words are inadequate to describe my incredible personal growth—despite numerous battles with doubt and fear— a deepening relationship with God . . . and countless testimonies of changed lives.

Adventuring with God has made my ordinary life fruitful.

God has designed us for fantastic adventure, and our deepest longings are his call to us to join him. There is nothing quite like adventuring with the God of the universe. I think of the void and regret I would feel had I stayed safe but captive. Who but God could reach so deep to touch my soul, truly satisfying my deepest longings? I know God so much better now.

The Spiritual S is a curve that depicts the natural cycle of your spiritual life. You may experience a sense of freedom simply by understanding the cycle. But how much more freeing when you know how to identify your place on the Spiritual S and use it to direct yourself to step or "Jump" to a deeper level of intimacy with God? Repeatedly, I found that a small jump on my Spiritual S (that is, moving into greater dependence on God) led to meaningful life-changing innovations in other areas. As I changed on the inside, God moved me to make changes to my work. No longer locked in a self-imposed prison, my Spiritual S Jumps unlocked the doors of my physical world. God gave me whole new reasons for how I used my time. He flipped my life upside down; I found myself free and fulfilled! The Spiritual S is the path leading to deeper intimacy with God, where life is free, our beliefs are aligned with God's, and we learn to transform how we use our time to make it fulfilling. It's a wonderful thing—and you can experience this.

What I have learned, observed and experienced is expressed here in a way I hope will be enlightening and give you a structure and language that will embolden you to pursue God's path to freedom and fulfillment. This book is a self-coaching tool to help you unlock your life and guide you into a life of freedom and meaning. In Part 1: The Foundation, I lay down the foundational concepts. For some, simply understanding these will bring a sense of peace and a framework to explain why you experience certain feelings and events. In Part 2: The Path, I expand on the concepts and build them into a practical Five-Step Mission Curve Process delineating the path to unlock your life. In Part 3: Guidance, I provide you with detailed exercises and tips to lead you to develop a specific plan for your life and put in place the structure to support yourself as you move forward. Here the rubber hits the road. You're only *Five Steps and a Jump!* away from launching your adventure!

It is most powerful to work through the exercises one at a time over several weeks or months as appropriate for your situation. The exercises and guidance are designed to liberate your thinking and empower you to move forward with confidence, conviction and support. You may benefit greatly by working through these with the help of a trusted coach, mentor or as part of a life group. Living a free and fulfilling life is not an event or end goal but movement along a path. If you are like me, you will go through the steps many times as you progress through the natural cycle of the S curve. Plan to build these concepts into your life so you will have the tools you need to continue to grow.

This process will help you embrace the adventure God has for you: an incredibly fruitful life, one you won't regret living.

Why do we love adventure stories? We long to be part of the story—and we are! We need only to break out of our self-inflicted prisons to embrace its fullness. Mastering your S curves leads to a life of deep intimacy and oneness with God himself. This is God's desire for you! He yearns for you to join him in his adventure so you will find life. It begins with one small step toward God on your Spiritual S.

The guiding principle of the Spiritual S is intimacy, the path to oneness with God. Intimacy creates intimacy, so I start with some of my testimony to illustrate the principles. It is my hope that you capture the sense that there is an exciting adventure awaiting you. There is a way out.

Part 1: The Foundation

The Fruits of Adventure

"Come and listen, all you who fear God, and I will tell you
what he did for me."   - King David, Psalm 66:16

My wife Sue and I remember a lingering sense that something was missing in our lives. Everything was ideal on paper: we had a young family and lived in a nice neighborhood in Syracuse, New York where I had a very good job. We thought of moving; change would be good, we'd gain more community. We just didn't fit in where we were—a bit stuck or out of place—and bored. Something eluded us. Life was good but not vibrant. We went house shopping in a neighboring town. But God had other plans.

Sue was raised as a Presbyterian so, like so many do, when the kids were little we began to attend a church just down the road. I didn't know much then about church and belief systems; I was raised Christian Scientist. One central and positive emphasis of Christian Science is faith, so I was quite comfortable in my belief in God. On the other hand, Christian Science does not teach that we need a savior or that Jesus came to save us. After a while the lights went on for me, and I decided to accept Jesus' offer of salvation and follow him. It felt like a step in the right direction. No fireworks or bells, but a small spark was ignited. Little did I know that it triggered the start of a life-changing adventure. God helped me to redeem the faith I had developed as a Christian Scientist by directing it to Christ, and my journey quietly began. Not long after, Sue encouraged me to join a men's group. This was about the same time we were wondering about moving. Reluctantly, I agreed—I might meet some good guys.

Our meeting one night is as clear to me if it were yesterday. We were doing an audio men's study hosted by Dennis Rainey. He challenged us to pray with our wives. "Are you kidding me?" I thought, "that would be weird at best." But we all left that night challenged and committed, knowing that the following week we'd have to check in. There was no way to evade the embarrassment of being the only guy not to. On the surface, it didn't seem like a big deal, but I knew this would push my envelope. I don't recall how I presented it to Sue when I got home, as an experiment, probably, not something ongoing. Prayer was awkward and uncomfortable for both of us. We prayed for a change in our lives, whether to move and to where, for God to address this sense of routine and void in our lives and to bring us into community. Despite the awkwardness, we prayed every night.

In the meantime, I had some major projects going on at work. I was involved with corporate mergers and acquisitions and we always had several irons in the fire. One project was a significant opportunity to acquire an Oregon-based company. In prior years, it had never seemed a good strategic fit; now, though, as the process moved toward a decision, the CEO of my company said to me, "I'd like you to move to Oregon to integrate this business with ours. Let me know your answer tomorrow." (It wasn't really a question.) Sue and I had 24 hours to decide. This happened a mere three weeks after we had started to pray together. It was immediately apparent to us that God was involved.

Praying with your spouse is powerful!

We bought a new house, sold our house and were in Oregon in just over two months. For Sue and me, both from the Midwest/East Coast, with our families still there, this was a major move, way off the radar. It went like clockwork, amazing considering the Syracuse real estate market. Shortly after we arrived in Oregon I sat in a park with Sue as the kids played, wondering if this was a mirage. It happened so fast, a blur! When God answered our prayers, it was powerful and swift. I clearly saw His hands all over this, and even more now, looking back.

When we arrived, fired up about God's answer to our prayer we sought a church. After rejecting a half dozen, we got a flyer in the mail inviting us to a new church in a nearby town, located in a school. "A school, really?" I said to Sue. I thought it bizarre—churches should meet in established buildings—but Sue wanted to check it out. I was intrigued: the church was three weeks old. After the service, we connected with the pastor. The "start-up" atmosphere resonated with my business experience. I soon found they needed us. The pastor, now my closest friend Brad, felt that

God "sent us." He had been praying for people to help him get this church off the ground. Another answered prayer! I got very involved, serving in various capacities as the church grew. I was on a great spiritual growth path kicked off by the clear leading to move to Oregon. God gave us a great community; no longer were we haunted by the sense that something was not right. Risking prayer together brought us closer to God, which led us to release what we had in Syracuse and launched us into a new exciting stage of our adventure.

Yet this was just the beginning.

My spiritual growth was accelerating. I was officially baptized that spring. Brad led me to begin each morning by dedicating an hour to reading the Bible, praying and journaling. Other than a verse here or there, I had never really read the Bible. The company merger had me traveling a lot and, on one trip, when I realized I had forgotten mine, I stopped at the airport bookstore and bought the only Bible they had, an edition with a structured reading plan from the Old and New Testaments, Proverbs and Psalms, to read the whole Bible in a year—I did not get to choose the topics. The simple switch to this new Bible felt odd but significant. Each day, the readings were totally relevant to my life! Later that day I would hear it again, or something else would connect me back to the scripture. It happened too often to be coincidence. I began to pay attention. "God, you must really want me to get this," I thought. I would proactively ask God, "What are you telling me in this Scripture?" The Bible came to life. Clearly the Holy Spirit was opening things up: my spiritual walk took on a new dimension.

Within two years, however, though busy and successful, as in Syracuse I again suffered from "been there, done that": things irritated me. At the company nearly 20 years, I knew the owners, the culture, the history. I could have remained there my entire life.

But could I?

I could stay the course, safe and secure. I have a family to provide for, a college education fund. Retirement, too. Endure, retire in 10–15 years, then do something else. Be prudent. Or, . . . jump ship and work for another business—I have a lot to offer! Or. . .? Struggling, I would get excited about the possibilities, only to be yanked back by the realities of my world. Financial security and responsibilities dominated me, held me captive.

One morning, praying after reading the parable of the talents, I had a vision of standing inside the courtyard of a fortress, looking out giant timbered gates down a winding trail through the grass into the woods. It looked beautiful and exciting, but disquieting. I looked back and forth between the trail in front of me and the fortress where I stood, wondering. The implication was clear. "Stay in the secure walls and endure the struggle like a prison sentence" vs. "Adventure down that beautiful trail, full of unknown threats and situations." Yikes! Intrigued by the adventure yet afraid to move, I had no idea what to do.

I now realize that God has instilled this desire in us to adventure with him. Through adventure he brings us close to himself, into intimacy, where true freedom resides.

I had begun to draw closer to God.

The desire for adventure stirred in me. Questions popped into my head. "Is there more to life than this? Am I really using all of my talents fully?" What to do? Run out the door? I wasn't ready for that. I needed to get myself moving. I poked around, exploring different possibilities. I talked to people in different fields, with different experiences. Almost two years considering, reflecting, praying, and talking to close friends. I spent a lot of time trying to understand. "Who did God make me to be? Why does he have me here, now?" I learned a lot about myself as I talked with God, hoping for answers. Tough conversations—God demands honesty. I admitted weaknesses and let go of unrealistic career aspirations—hard but freeing. I learned more about my unique strengths, which ultimately revealed the "Character Identity" that captures the specific role God wired me to play. I had to choose to build on my strengths and experiences but also stretch by doing things I was uncomfortable doing. God also put on my heart that my path would need to be more meaningful. Why else would I consider changing?

Being financially risk-averse, the thought of leaving my job of 20+ years was worrying. Was I nuts? What ultimately got to me was the answer to this question: "Do I want to do what I am doing for the rest of my life?"

I realized that while my company did some noble work, it was not really helping people face major problems. There was a greater work for me. I was changing. I wanted to hear, "Well done, good and faithful servant." Idling in a fortress just didn't fit. God wanted me on the front lines, helping others. He was leading me to make a major "Jump." I would give up a lot to move ahead. Moreover, I had to confront my financial insecurities and surrender to God's leadership. Gut wrenching!

I did what I could to prepare. Remembering my days of backpacking, I realized if I were to venture down the trail, I had better not carry much. Too much weight would slow me down and limit my agility. "Travel Light," I heard in my mind. I spent a lot of time lightening our financial situation in preparation for the Jump. We downsized our house and I set aside some money in reserve.

After exploring several options, I decided to be a financial advisor, a massive change. (Sue still can't believe she let me do this. I have an awesome wife.) My starting income would drop 75%. I would be on commission with no steady paychecks. Sue did not have a full-time job, just part-time work from home. With young kids, bills etc. this was quite scary, made more so because growing up, my family had struggled financially, even living on food stamps for a while. My parents had fought about money occasionally; I would run the other way. Apparently, an unspoken vow has caused me to passionately avoid money issues.

A crazy thought—I could help other people to likewise avoid them. Yet here I was confronting my own insecurity head on. I felt God with me, but I wasn't totally sure. I just needed to go forward to try to help people.

I did not want to be the typical financial advisor. Reflecting on who God made me to be and do, I realized people's financial and spiritual lives lie close beside each other. Money often becomes a god, a source of security and provision. It's so easy to put more faith in our money than in God, the source of it all. I thought that somehow, while helping people with their money issues, I might have the opportunity to touch on spiritual matters with them. Also, I perceived that my fear of financial challenges had kept me from exploring other possibilities for my life, things I might have really enjoyed doing.

When I was feeling stuck in my job I noticed many others who seemed stuck too. I asked myself, "Why aren't they getting out?" I expect money issues were a big factor holding them hostage. Just ask someone what they would do if they won ten million dollars and you'll see. The idea came to me to "help free people financially, so they can do what they are meant to do with their lives." Little did I know that this was the beginnings of my Life Mission. My work life was transformed; it gained meaning, focus and purpose, the result of first making changes in my spiritual life. My work would become a far greater work, now with my gifts, abilities and passion all aligned with God's.

I got my nerve up, and set out to leave my job of 21 years. The support I received from my closest friends, my team, believers who had helped me along the way was vital. Most importantly, Sue was apprehensive but very supportive; without her, I never would have made it. I think she knew intuitively that God would take care of us. On the other hand, some friends thought I was crazy. One said I was "too nice a guy" to be a financial advisor. He wished me luck. (Ouch!) When I resigned, my boss said, "You might do that for a year or two and then will be back." Another vote of "confidence"! It is so common, even expected, when stepping out, to be hit by "Vision Killers," often from those closest to you. Hits like this seem to go below the belt; though not intended to, innocent comments can stop you in your tracks. You can guess the source of these. If not for my faith in God, and the support of my team, I could well have bailed on the plan. But I had key disciplines, Life Mission and support to keep me going. My highest priority was to help people get free; financial advising came second.

Through all of this, God has poured out his blessing beyond my wildest expectations. Joining God in adventure produces incredible fruit. I've enjoyed helping countless people open up new stages of their lives. I've seen people change careers and others venture out as missionaries, so many totally transformed. What a blessing to have shared the journey with them! At the same time,

I've had to do things I did not like, labored through fiery trials and even encountered the threat of illness following rejection. I can tell countless stories of God's sovereignty, blessings and amazing provision; times of closeness with God, times of drifting away from God, then coming back to him again. I have let go of false beliefs about myself and confronted my biggest fears. So much I thought was important I now realize is not. All this has contributed to an ever-deepening spiritual intimacy with God and the freedom and fulfillment that come with it.

I learned something significant.

"Aha!"

"But it was to us that God revealed these things by his Spirit. For his Spirit searches out everything and shows us God's deep secrets."
The Apostle Paul – 1 Corinthians 2:10

Have you ever been oblivious to the undercurrents in a situation, and then later thought, "Aha! Now I know what was going on"? This has happened to me many, many times. I look back to get a broader look, put the pieces together, and perhaps see a pattern.

A few years ago, reflecting over the adventure of my last 25 years, my mind drifted back to when Sue and I were in Syracuse feeling we needed a change, yet the solutions we thought could fix things were a bit off base. Years later, again restless and trapped, longing for something. Immediately after moving to Oregon: new role at work, new home, new community; everything fresh. I was learning and growing so much, it was fun! After I made the jump to financial advisor: overwhelmed but excited! I asked myself, "What is going on in all this? Is there a pattern that would help explain what I was going through?"

Thinking over patterns I knew, it hit me like a ton of bricks. "Aha! I know this pattern!" My life would never be the same. My life track paralleled a concept I learned in business school. I was following the pattern of the S Curve.

My first job was as an engineer developing new medical devices. I really enjoyed bringing new products to the marketplace. That I could participate in helping the company grow the business and set a direction for its future intrigued me. I decided to get an MBA and focus my classwork on bringing new product innovations to the market. In school I learned all about product lifecycle curves, which describe the stages of a product's life from concept to launch, growth, maturity, decline and finally obsolescence.

I'm sure you can relate to this familiar pattern as you think about products you have used. A new product comes to market, everybody buys one, eventually everyone has one and sales drop, perhaps due to competition, so the company discontinues the product. In business, the lifecycle curves are often called S curves based on the characteristic shape of the front portion. Business leaders understand these cycles so as a product matures through its lifecycle, they make plans to launch a next generation product or new product innovation to expand sales, typically with a corresponding plan to obsolete the older product. The launch of the new product is called an S-curve "Jump" because it boosts the business to a new level, keeping it alive and growing.

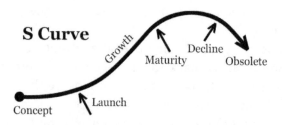

Think of Apple. Originally a PC company, innovation Jumps transformed the company, first with the iPod (Music) and then the iPhone, as they sought to more completely serve its customers. In the process, Apple's new products led to the downfall of CDs and older model cell phones. Innovation always leads to obsolescence. If a business fails to innovate, its downfall is just a matter of time. On the other hand, a healthy business will go through this process of launching new products proactively as it grows and responds to competition. With each product launch (Jump), the company furthers its growth and, in so doing, defines and refines its unique purpose for being in business: its mission, the path the company follows to bring value to its shareholders as it serves its customers in a greater way.

The company's mission is its reason for being.

Going back to Apple. Steve Job's original mission was "to make a contribution to the world by making tools that advance humankind." See how the new products led to the fulfillment of Apple's mission? Well-run companies proactively define their mission based on their core values (where they have been, competitive forces, where they are and where they want to go) and then plan product generations to pursue it. The mission's powerful purpose is to focus and align the power of the organization to support the mission. It brings life. A company without a mission will not thrive, having no reason for being. Apple remains focused and has thrived, aligning the entire organization around fulfilling its mission.

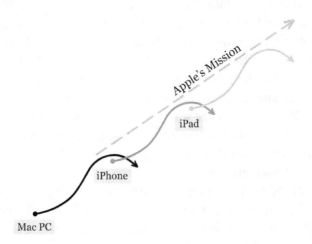

My Aha! Our lack of community in Syracuse was the later stage of just such a curve—no longer growing but bored and stagnating, like a lackluster product, we were trapped in the end of this stage of life.

Our move to Oregon was a major Jump of our S curve, bringing us back onto the upward slope when we were rapidly growing again. Exciting! Just like when a new product is brought to market. We experienced innovation and rapid growth, launching a new stage of life. Transformed. This and my subsequent career change consisted of a series of S-curve Jumps, like those when companies expand their business by launching new products.

We thrived when we made Jumps; we gained a reason for being.

What was different, however, is that I noticed the change on multiple levels, not only external changes (new jobs) but also transformations within me. The physical changes were obvious— how I used my time before and after the Jumps. When I left Syracuse, though I still spent most of my time working, it was fresh new work that challenged me. Later, my new career forced me to learn a whole new business, financial advising. Literally everything from when I went to work until I went to bed was different. These visible changes are what most of us see when we make a change. This represents one S curve I call the "Works S." It applies to where we focus our time, skills and resources, where the world can see who we are and what we do. Works S Jumps carry a significant material cost: they require the release of another significant part of your life. Moving to Oregon meant leaving Syracuse. To leave my old career. A Works S Jump calls for replacing old work with new. I immediately saw the importance of the Works S.

Our Works S is where we display our reason for being.

Yet a deep search of my soul and spirit revealed a significant and even more powerful change going on, a whole spiritual side that also followed an S curve.

I'd joined that men's group and was challenged to pray with my wife. Praying together really stretched us both spiritually. Not only did we have to follow through, but it raised the question "Why pray together if we don't think it will make a difference?" Did we really think God could do something for us? Plus, we were awkward in a way you wouldn't expect of a couple married almost ten years. We had to be more intimate. This was an S Jump spiritually. Praying together changed outdated beliefs into new ones. Like all Jumps, this cost us, but not materially.

Three weeks later when the opportunity to move to Oregon surfaced, we clearly saw it as an answer to prayer. Great spiritual growth came from this adventure. Closeness to God like I had never felt shaped our whole view of the move. This made the Works S Jump (deciding to move) much easier. Praying together was a precursor to my Works S Jump.

Prior to my career change, I initiated new spiritual disciplines including daily Bible reading, prayer, and journaling. Twice I also took a day in solitude dedicated to prayer and fasting. During these times I wrestled with big questions, such as "Why am I here?" and "Who am I, really?" During these times, I moved even closer to God and started to get answers to the questions. Again my beliefs changed. I had to get honest and let go of false beliefs about myself as well as my career aspirations. I realized God did not make me for the roles I aspired to. By releasing these, I could be true to myself and pursue new ideas for my life. Praying together triggered my Works S Jump; likewise, my new spiritual disciplines heralded a Works S Jump to financial advising. Each time I came closer to God, I was transformed internally. I was following the pattern of the Spiritual S curve. This was powerful.

While your Works S captures where you focus your time and resources, your Spiritual S captures your relationship with God deepening into intimacy, trust, and honesty, where beliefs are transformed. Both follow the same S shape: origination followed by growth, then leveling off followed by decline. Just as work becomes old and stale, our relationship with God can become dry and distant. Both can be rejuvenated by Jumps. In addition, the Works S and the Spiritual S are powerfully interconnected. With each rejuvenating Spiritual S Jump, my relationship with God deepened, becoming significantly more intimate. Due to this intimacy my beliefs changed, and God led me to make life changing Jumps on my Works S—outward changes that reflected transformational internal changes.

Understanding these S curves has helped me appreciate and gain perspective and comfort about happenings in my life. Most powerful for me is that, just as knowing the law of gravity helps scientists do things previously unimaginable, knowing the pattern of the S curves helps me do greater things with my life, and I feel freer and more fulfilled than I could ever have imagined.

This opportunity is available to everyone who is willing. It all begins by taking a seemingly small step to draw closer to God. Specifically, making a Jump on your Spiritual S leads to freedom and fulfillment.

Consider one person's experience to see how this worked in her life. (See sidebar.) Of course, few will become a missionary like Jane. Your adventure will be unique and suited to yourself. It's not something to be feared; it will be very exciting for you!

Jane (not her real name) was a successful educator in a health-related field. About 12 years ago she felt moved to go on a medical mission trip to Africa with an organization she found through her church. Already a faithful person, she felt this might be a good use of her medical skills. Seeing the suffering of the people, the children, and their hunger for God significantly changed her. She realized life was not just about her. Coming back convicted that she could do a greater work, she planned to relocate to Africa to serve the needy. She diligently dedicated her life to annual trips to Africa and changed her entire financial world to save and prepare so she would have sufficient income to support herself without a job. Now, after incredible health and other challenges, miracles, and staying steadfastly focused, she lives there nearly year-round. She tells countless unbelievable stories of changed lives. Transformed, she has incredible intimacy with God and lives a free and fulfilling life. That first step, going on the mission trip (Spiritual S Jump), brought her closer to God, leading to significant changes in the rest of her life (Works S Jumps).

My "Aha" moment set my mind awhirl. All sorts of thoughts careened through my head. "There is more to this, something powerful, I need to figure out what it is." I had to understand these curves better. One by one the pieces came together. A framework emerged and as I grappled with it, I was struck—this is the basis for answering life's biggest questions! The way to unlock your life. The way to live the life you were meant to live, a life you will not regret. The answers emerged from a deeper understanding of the relationship between the Works S and Spiritual S.

We'll go through the principles here, but everything will hit home as you read through the Path and then follow the Guidance, implementing the Five-Step Process and launching the adventure of your life.

It's time.

Work, Inspired!

The Lord God placed the man in the Garden of Eden to
tend and watch over it.   *Genesis 2:15*

Work is the place where you spend significant time, energy and resources doing things out in the world. Clearly God planned for us to work from the beginning when he placed Adam and Eve in the garden to tend it and reign over the earth, and he declared it good. Yet since the fall of man, work has been corrupted and can become a burden or an addiction. Many of us run away from work and find excuses for doing nothing. Others are so obsessed with work they are literally killing themselves (I can relate to this!). Nor is working like crazy to retire so you can play all the time God's plan; he doesn't call us to sit back and take it easy. The parable of Bigger Barns tells us this. All these stem from the brokenness we live in. Regardless of where you fall in this spectrum, God calls all of us to work because he knows that work is an essential part of a vibrant and fulfilling life. We don't necessarily need to be paid for our work, God simply wants us contributing. He has gifted each of us with unique skills and abilities to do good works with the intent to serve others. In God's clever way, work provides on multiple levels. In addition to financial benefits, as we contribute to the world we gain social and emotional rewards, giving us a sense of purpose and connection. Work is how we live out God's adventure for our lives.

Work helps fulfill a deep desire God planted in our hearts. He designed us to participate by pursuing a specific purpose as part of a community. Our work is one of the most significant contributors—or, misaligned, detriments—to finding our sense of fulfillment. We spend so much time at work. We must figure out our unique role. The question arises, "Why am I here?" I believe God raises this question in us so that we seek his answer—and it's wonderful to know he has one! He reveals it to us when we are honest with him as we pursue deeper intimacy along the Spiritual S. (More on this later.)

As we undertake our work, we follow the pattern of the Works S, which has the characteristic S-shaped curve. It helps to adjust the language a little to make it more work specific. Most people first engage their Works S as they pursue their occupation or career after they graduate from school and enter the workforce. The Works S "launches" when you take a job. In your new position, you learn fresh skills to become more proficient in your work; this is often a time of excitement, challenge, opportunity, and rapid growth. This is not necessarily an easy time; in fact, you will be stressed as you learn new skills and processes. Over time, however, you become competent and efficient as you settle in.

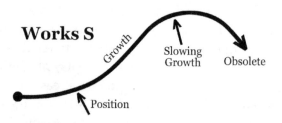

If you stay in the same job long enough, you may get a little bored or complacent as your growth slows and you approach the peak of your Works S. You may feel "Stuck! Something is missing; there has to be more for me than this!" You find yourself weighing the alternatives of staying put versus changing jobs, as you follow the curve's decline. If you're like me, you struggle with the uneasy prospect of leaving the secure, comfortable, and familiar. The decision holds you hostage as your fears convince you you're better off where you are. Debilitating apathy and waning passion lessens your influence. You complain more or focus on outside diversions. Some spend a large part of their lives "comfortable in their discontent," idle and stagnant, inhibiting achievement of their full potential, as their agility diminishes. Others become outmoded as the industry changes. Reasons abound as to why someone may become obsolete, adrift, unsure what to do.

Whether change is imposed or you preemptively explore opportunities, inevitably you must make a Jump on your Works S to start a new cycle and get back on the growth slope, perhaps by landing a new position or even starting a new career. But what will inspire your Jump? Selfish motives (provision, fame, fortune, comfort, power, challenge or change for its own sake) alone? Or will you engage God and let him inspire you? I contend that by leaving God out of the picture, you miss out on true fulfillment. Many a man has attained worldly success only to find his life hollow, mere existence. Think on the words of the wealthy writer of Ecclesiastes:

> But as I looked at everything I had worked so hard to accomplish, it was all so meaningless—like chasing the wind. There was nothing really worthwhile anywhere."
> *Ecclesiastes 12:1*

When God instills in us the desire to pursue a purpose in our community, he intends it to be rich and fulfilling, not draining, not hollow. Think how many fail to live this out!

God, like a company shareholder, wants you to stretch, to explore, to break free, to reach your full potential as you serve him by serving people. How? By making God-inspired Jumps on your Works S, which follow intimacy deepening Jumps on your Spiritual S. And just as a thriving company has a company mission, you, too, can have a "Life Mission," your reason for being and source of fulfillment. You will thrive when you live out your mission in increasing intimacy with God, maximizing your value, usefulness, and unique contributions. A sense of fulfillment permeates each of us as we pursue our mission. Incredible!

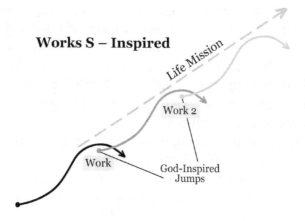

Works S – Inspired

Life Mission

Work 2

Work

God-Inspired
Jumps

Much more to come about Life Missions. You will draft your Life Mission in the exercises in Part 3: Guidance. This will power your life. You can thrive!

My friend Jeff, significantly hit financially by the recession, decided to make a career change but ended up in a position that just was not a good fit. Clearly, he was struggling in the later stages of his Works S (stuck, out of place). Jeff connected most intimately with God when hiking, so God inspired him to go every week (Spiritual S Jump). He joined an organization that trains volunteers to search for lost hikers. This, along with identifying the key strengths and passions he had displayed throughout his life, proved he was gifted at "helping people navigate complex high consequence situations" (the beginning of his Life Mission). He could help, whether a lost hiker or a business owner navigating a complex financial world. He realized he couldn't fulfill his mission where he was working, so he took a position at a company better suited to serve business owners. Now he is thriving (though it's still early on) and has even aligned his passion for hiking with his business, arranging adventure hikes for his clients.

Your Inspiration?

If you openly declare that Jesus is Lord and believe in your heart that God raised him from the dead, you will be saved. For it is by believing in your heart that you are made right with God, and it is by openly declaring your faith that you are saved.

The Apostle Paul – Romans 10:9–10

From birth, we naturally seek our own worldly self-interest, unmindful of others. The world is our reference as we bounce from one trendy belief to another, navigating as best we can based on things we hear or people we meet. It's easy for financial success, material possessions, sexual love, fame, or even our good name to drive us. We rule over our lives. Some claim to be spiritual and live a moral life but serve no god outside themselves. Perhaps they just have a good moral compass, as did I. Before giving my life to Christ, I would have said I believed in God, yet in the end I was my own god. Ultimately, I realized this approach to life just did not work. I did not recognize the void deep inside but, unawares, I was searching, approaching the Spiritual S. We seek spiritual solutions for answers to life's big questions: Why do I feel this way? What's missing? Isn't there more to life? Why did this happen? Shouldn't this get better? What am I supposed to do?

Something working in and around me made me realize I had a decision to make: to stay this course (using the ways of the world as my belief system and basis for decisions) or to admit this wasn't viable and decide to follow and be inspired by a higher spiritual power. To follow God, I had to give up my own way and follow him ("Surrender"). To accept Jesus Christ as my savior and surrender leadership to him, to launch the Spiritual S, to be born again—an irreversible and life-changing event if a person is sincere—by both declaring with my lips and believing in my heart, as Paul said. Like me, each of you has this same decision to make, though many never give it much thought. In his infinite wisdom, God has given us the freedom to choose what or whom we want to follow; he cannot (or will not) mandate that we love him. We must choose.

Surrendering leadership to Jesus is the foundation for many future surrenders. To comprehend this is most humbling. It is not simply a change, like getting that first job on the Works S; we can always get another job and start over. Not so with this decision, which instigates the transformation of your life. This can be a scary proposition. There is no turning back if you truly make this surrender. It alters the whole basis on which you live your life. This did not come easy for me. Who wants to surrender? "I've been a pretty good guy after all. Why should I have to give up? Only wimps surrender, right?" I thought. To surrender is unnatural. When surrounded, we fight or run. Confronted with this choice, some fight, coming up with a litany of reasons for why they can't accept Christ or believe in God. Perhaps they are afraid they will have to give up having fun. Others hide under an umbrella, calling themselves Christians since they were raised in church. Alas, being born into a Christian family does not make a person a Christian. Sadly, many fall into the latter category, mouthing the words yet uncommitted at heart, following the ways of the world but with a Christian façade, like a person boarding a train but keeping one foot on the platform. It doesn't work. Me, I was living a moral life with no true basis. I had never really heard the gospel. When it finally sank in, my life began to change, one surrender at a time, after this first and most significant.

What a struggle it was.

To surrender requires a leap of faith, but in what or whom? Faith is believing in someone you can't see, Jesus. How can you know beforehand this is the gateway to a free, full life? My friend Lee tells an amazing story of his search for meaning, culminating in a deep faith and close walk with God, so close that he wrestles with how to let others know how good it can be: "How can one who has seen a sunset explain it to a blind person?"

All I can say is that each of us must take a chance, step out in faith and look for ourselves. What if it is true? Let yourself go, you will not feel yourself being caught until you do. You cannot let go and hold on with the other hand. Surrendering always requires faith, letting go of the old, reaching forward to the new. Have you made a decision both with your lips and in your heart to surrender your life to Jesus?

If your answer is "Yes!" welcome to the Spiritual S. You are born again to a life of freedom, you are a new person. Now it's time to learn what this means. It's time to grow into your newfound freedom, like a baby maturing into an adult.

> *This means that anyone who belongs to Christ has*
> *become a new person. The old life is gone; a new life has*
> *begun!*   The Apostle Paul – 2 Corinthians 5:17

Having accepted Christ, you will experience growth as you explore and learn. Moving up the slope of the Spiritual S we are drawn closer to God as we begin to believe and follow what he teaches. I call this slope Intimacy because we become more dependent on God and lean on him for support. We need him! We trust him so we can let go of false beliefs about ourselves or him. God transforms our thinking. Miraculously, in Intimacy you also become contagious as you testify to others and draw them in. You're passionate! You're hungry, even desperate for him. Your testimony is pure. You find yourself changing to become more like God. Your life is bearing fruit you perhaps won't even realize.

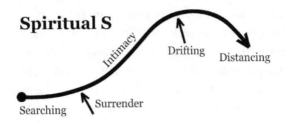

Though not always comfortable (growth can be painful), I love this stage. I say, "Wouldn't it be great if I could stay here forever?" Then I find myself drifting as routine settles in and my exciting growth fades. It's entrenched in our Spiritual S. Following the curve, we stagnate, our faith declines, we grow less intimate with and more independent of God: we no longer are living to our full potential. We grow distant. This is as true now, though more mature, as when I first believed. The S curve runs its course.

What happens next differs for each of us, however. Many stall on the decline of the curve. Others re-engage as they seek for God to play the lead in their life. In the parable (found in Matthew), Jesus tells how a seed planted in good soil (a believer) produces 100, or 60, or 30 times the fruit. God does not expect us all to produce the same amount, but he does want us to reach our full fruit-bearing potential, relying heavily on and transformed to be more like him, not adrift on the downward slope, far from him, barren, where the complacent end up.

A Spiritual S Jump is required to produce more fruit.

God loves it when we initiate the Jump onto a new upslope, entering into a fresh, deeper level of Intimacy. But occasionally, unfruitful for too long, we discern a nudge, a change he allows in our lives or the unpleasant aftereffects of a decision.

> *"I am the true grapevine, and my Father is the gardener. He cuts off every branch of mine that doesn't produce fruit, and he prunes the branches that do bear fruit so they will produce even more."*
> *Jesus Christ – John 15:1–2*

What God most desires is us. Not wanting us to settle, if need be, he will move us. He loves us and wants intimacy culminating in oneness, the deepest of relationships. Perhaps unconsciously, we want this too—to be unconditionally loved, free to be ourselves. When we are intimate with God we trust and depend on him, our beliefs are reshaped, and he helps us see what he made us to be and do. Then we produce incredible fruit.

Whether self-initiated or the result of some event, intimacy-deepening Jumps on our Spiritual S lead us to accept God's guidance, including the direction of our Works S and Life Mission. Inspired, each Works S Jump stretches our faith to see God act. We gain more and more confidence as we are freed to be the person God meant us to be. Emboldened, we go further in the next cycle of our S curves. But there is a catch.

... I have come that they may have life, and have it to the full.   *Jesus Christ – John 10:10*

Jesus came to free us and lead us to fully live. Nevertheless, though born again, we cling to our old world, fearful infants, like my daughter who, when first learning to swim, anxiously clung to the side of the pool. It took courage and trust to let go and swim to me. God loves us so much he calls us to let go, yet we struggle to overcome our fears. It's all about truth vs. lies, an incredible battle. But we can go to God, seeking the truth about who he is and who we are. When we do this God releases us from the chains that bind us.

When we draw closer to God (a Spiritual S Jump), he asks us to surrender what holds us fast, to bring the lies into the light. Surrendering is painful, but how often have I said, "I should have done this long ago"? Nothing beats letting go and finding freedom. But like first accepting Christ as Lord of your life, surrender is unnatural. We fight it with all our strength. But to grow closer to God, we must get used to it. To grow, something must first die. With each pass through, God asks us to release another lie.

You now have the framework of the Works S and Spiritual S and the powerful interdependency between them. Following a move by us to deepen intimacy with God (Spiritual S Jump), he inspires us, affirming who we are, to make changes in what we do (Works S Jump). With each cycle of the Spiritual S our beliefs become more like God's; we move toward oneness with him. With each cycle of the Works S, God-inspired Jumps define our Life Mission, our source of fulfillment. As we pursue this, we produce wonderful fruit for the kingdom of God which fuels our next cycle. Together, the curves reveal the answers to life's biggest questions. *There is hope for us!*

It is good to know what the cycles look like. Perhaps you're already reflecting on the curves and now have a new perspective on your life. Understanding your past is fine, but imagine how knowing your place on the curves could proactively keep you on the powerful slopes of Growth (Works S) and Intimacy (Spiritual S). It is so much better to pursue adventure than to get moved!

Fortunately, God has built into us some helpful mechanisms, our emotions, which create tension useful in navigating our curves and directing us into adventure. We must know where we are before we know where to place our next step. The stakes are high!

As you read through the next section, see if you can figure out where you are right now on your Works and Spiritual S curves. Are you Locked In?

Locked In?

"For God has not given us a spirit of fear and timidity, but of power, love, and self-discipline."
The Apostle Paul – 2 Timothy 1:7

It's so easy to ride the roller coaster of our varied emotions as we react to events. I'm always amazed at what goes on in my mind. Curiously, often I'm depressed just after a big success. Immediately I worry over what's next. Or, I get so busy that I pray for a break, and then when I get one, I feel anxiety and guilt for being lax.

Emotions and feelings help us understand, but if we let them lead, we go astray. Rightly used, emotions are a thermometer; they give the temperature without telling us what to do. We get to decide whether we wear a coat. God has given us a spirit of power, love and self-discipline so we can objectively take our emotional temperature and decide how to respond. Our emotions should not control us.

S curves provide a reference to keep emotions in perspective. We experience "Emotional Tensions" as we are pulled back and forth by both positive and negative emotions at the various stages. This causes conflict within us but helps us gauge where we are and explains why we feel a certain way. Recognizing the Emotional Tensions we are experiencing can be comforting in the midst of seesawing back and forth.

While we don't want our emotions to control us, they can either hinder or energize a change, so we want to know how to utilize them wisely. One of my favorite sayings is, "What you focus on increases." Fear easily becomes our focus, and it grows. Fear is the primary reason why people remain stuck on the downslope of their S curves. We must manage our focus. Knowing your place on the S curves builds passion by channeling your emotional energy in the right direction to keep fear in its place. God makes it clear that he has not given us a spirit of fear and timidity. He calls us to lean forward in life, in power, love and self-discipline. Our emotions are a tool and perhaps an asset, but not a guide. We must retain control.

Let's look at some of the common Emotional Tensions of the stages of the S curve. What are you experiencing now?

Emotional Tensions

Clearly, while restless in Syracuse Sue and I were entering the Decline stage. A move might relieve the tension but also shake us from our comfortable nest. In Portland, everything was in Growth. New, fresh, exciting; nail-biting. The excitement, the adventure far outweighed the fear. Our energy level was flying high. Exploring, working hard, learning about ourselves, spiritually growing, and very enthusiastic—we were alive! And contagious. A great time.

A few years later, again my enthusiasm for work had waned. Life was routine ("been there, done that"). Things irritated me. *Do I want to do this the rest of my life?* Secure, I craved more. Escape, but do what? Could I afford a change, with a young family and college costs coming? I distracted myself from the tension with exercise and long lunches. Clearly on the Decline again.

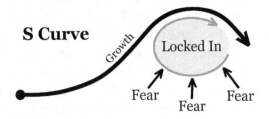

Petrified of leaving the financial and emotional stability of my job, I was at a fork in the road, but I could not seem to move, I was "Locked In." Trapped by the Emotional Tension of the Decline stage, I knew I had to change something.

> *My enemy has chased me. He has knocked me to the*
> *ground and forces me to live in darkness like those in the*
> *grave. I am losing all hope; I am paralyzed with fear.*
> *King David – Psalm 143:3-4*

King David paints a great word picture that captures the emotional tension of the last couple years of my former career. I felt paralyzed by fear, history, expectations. Perhaps you can relate. Are you tired, complacent, dull, frustrated, burdened, bored? We all feel this way now and then. Depleted, we need to replenish our souls and restore a proper balance. Maybe it's more. A much-needed break fails to rejuvenate, and you return as if you never left? Stuck due to circumstances? Disconnected? Out of place, with something missing? A mismatch for your job? Disappointed with where you are? Fixated on escaping your situation, you want out but are convinced you're just dreaming, unrealistic? Masking over discontent? Barely hanging on? Wasting away or dying? "There must be more to life than this?!"

Take some time, step back, and ask, "Am I living a vibrant fulfilling life?"

Many, many people I have met are Locked In, though most are unconscious of it. It's easy to suppress the feelings; duty overpowers them. Often, we convince ourselves just to endure our prison sentence Locked In, counting the days to "freedom." One guy told me he only had to endure his job for another 3 years, 127 days before he could retire. My heart felt his pain. We easily settle into discomfort; disliking where we are but used to it. We buy into the belief that the devil we know is better than the devil we don't.

We make excuses for why we stay. Jesus asks a sick man at the pool if he wants to get well, and he says: "I have been waiting for someone to help me into the water at the right time." Trapped for 38 years! I ask people who are Locked In, "Do you want to get out?" They say, "Yes! But. . ." and list reasons why they can't. Watch out! This is not where God wants you, and when you get out of your prison, you'll realize that it's not where you want to be ever again if you can help it. This is the stage of the S curve to be most wary of; it is not a place you should linger. Keep an eye out for the telltale emotional tensions. Be honest with yourself! It's so important to know your place on your S curves.

Emotional Tensions by Stage

Conceptualization

Excited, energized, optimistic, creative, adventurous

Anxious, scared, unsure, self-doubting, self-deprecating, self-critical, making excuses

Growth

Challenged, energized, invigorated, stretched, focused, just-do-it attitude, hungry

Lacking confidence, overwhelmed, stressed

Declining Growth

Competent, confident, mature, comfortable

Not challenged, wondering, bored at times, habitual

Decline

Stable, secure, predictable

Tired, unenthusiastic, apathetic, disconnected, feeling unimportant, trapped, just want to escape, out of place, increasing diversions, "been there, done that"

If you're Locked In, you're not alone; all of us find ourselves there many times. It is inherent to life. Subtly and gradually—as the fervor wanes—this stage sneaks up on us, following one of vibrant and intense growth when we relish well-deserved rewards for all our hard work. We're still growing, but our nature leads us to strive for comfort, and we, becoming more self-reliant, slide into Decline. Circumstances, experiences, and expectations (our own, and others of us) fester and trap us. Past decisions, even if they felt right at the time, strengthen the trap. Think of how a financial decision such as taking on a bigger mortgage or buying a fancier car comes back on us and restricts our flexibility due to the burden of debt. We must sustain our level of income, inhibiting change. We end up handcuffed to our job to serve our debt obligations. Proverbs 22 hits this point:

> *Just as the rich rule the poor, so the borrower is servant*
> *to the lender.*   – *Proverbs 22:7*

Unfortunate (for some, self-inflicted) circumstances have put many in a financial hole, resulting in living paycheck to paycheck, Locked In their job—trapped—just to survive.

Perhaps what traps us is not money but a potential loss of social status or reputation. Having risen through the ranks, change threatens. Ever heard the saying, "He's been promoted to the level of his incompetence"? This describes a man in the wrong spot, making his workers disgruntled and causing himself silent misery, who figures he had better hang on because he'll never reach this level again.

Maybe you are like I was, reasoning that while you are good at what you do, there is something more meaningful out there, which will make a bigger difference in the world. It's as if you're not playing in the real game. You sense God wants you to get moving, but with no idea what to do, you are scared to death to think about a change. Copious factors lead to becoming Locked In. Whatever the cause, the trap slowly deepens as rituals settle in. Past decisions and circumstances mount up, forming walls of fear that loom larger and larger, and we get stuck, perhaps comfortable but stagnating and unhappy—Locked In. Something must change.

We may intuitively sense that we are at a big fork in the road: "What should I do? Endure my sentence, or figure out how to escape?" If you serve your time, you may say to yourself, "It's not that bad really, I can tolerate it for a few more years." You also may notice that you escape along the way to temporarily relieve or distract yourself with drink or other obsessive behaviors, only to find yourself back in the trap a short time later. We look down the other path and dream about a better situation someday; adventure calls us, but it seems so unattainable.

You sense there is more to life than this, but you feel helpless, with no way out. It looks like a big blank piece of paper in front of us. "What could I do? How? What if I fail? How am I supposed to handle it financially? What will people think? Am I a wimp, giving up?" We might even reach a point of defeat and say, "I could never do something like that." Our fears are very good at holding us hostage! A little negative voice likes to whisper in our ear. Voices of others, often those closest to us, reinforce our doubts.

No wonder we get paralyzed! We spiral down, absent zest or passion, till we give up and slide into disappointed obsolescence. I've been there a few times myself. Is this how it has to be? At times we might need briefly to endure being Locked In, but "until we retire"? The rest of our lives? At what price? Someone once said, "Time is your most precious asset; we all get the same 24 hours a day, 7 days a week. We need to be very careful how we spend it." Think about where your time goes. How long does God give us here, anyway? If time is your most precious asset, is it wasting away? We sit at the crossroads with a choice to make:

This is what the Lord says: "Stop at the crossroads and look around. Ask for the old, godly way, and walk in it. Travel its path, and you will find rest for your souls. But you reply, 'No, that's not the road we want!'
Jeremiah 6:16

When we are Locked In, there is no rest for our souls. It may not seem so, but there is a way out that leads to a life lived to the fullest, the path to unlocking your life. I know because I have been on that path, and it's worth the trip. Having broken free a few times, I can say how vibrant my life has become and how much I have grown through the process of innovating my life.

> *The temptations in your life are no different from what others experience. And God is faithful. He will not allow the temptation to be more than you can stand. When you are tempted, he will show you a way out so that you can endure.* The Apostle Paul – 1 Corinthians 10:13

The truth is that I am no more special to God than you are. We all have a unique set of circumstances that leads us to become Locked In. God wants each of us set free, so he always shows the way out, but we must choose it. I coached a woman who did.

Sarah (not her real name) had had a troubled childhood. She felt she did not fit in, an outcast of sorts. She rebelled, ran off when she was 16 and ended up in a homosexual lifestyle. After many years, she started to question her life and felt led to go to church (Spiritual S Jump). She started to change on the inside and realized that she had become Locked In—trapped in her lifestyle. She pursued her faith diligently and decided to change her life (Works S Jump). Being Catholic, she thought to become a monastic nun but was declined. But she began to see this rejection as a blessing. She started to work with children and youth and found she gravitated toward the outcasts. She is finding her Life Mission is to serve those who are outcasts, just as she had felt growing up.

Incredible!

When we are Locked In, standing at the crossroads, we must take a step toward the "Old, Godly Way." A Spiritual S Jump. Sarah's life was transformed by taking that step, and the good news is that yours can be too. There is a way out, and it is worth the trip!

Jesus is asking you the same question he asked the man at the pool: "Do you want to get well?"

The Old, Godly Way

*"My thoughts are nothing like your thoughts," says
the Lord. "And my ways are far beyond anything you
could imagine. For just as the heavens are higher than the
earth, so my ways are higher than your ways and my
thoughts higher than your thoughts."*   Isaiah 55:8–9

Who wouldn't choose the path that Jeremiah says leads you to find rest for your soul? Sure, sounds good! But what does this mean? What do I do? How do I do it? Incessant questions spring to mind, and before you know it you are overwhelmed again by the same fears that have you Locked In. No progress! But God always gives us a path, a portal, or a crack to crawl through. His ways are not our ways; often the path is not where we are looking. We want something clearly laid out in front of us so it is easy to weigh the risks and make a logical decision. In Syracuse, when Sue and I felt empty, our first thought was to find a new community. We looked for a new house within our budget and all that goes with it.

That's the way the world works; it feels natural to us. When Locked In on our Works S, right away we look for the solution on the Works S, something better. Problem at work? Get a new job. Problem with a relationship? Get a new relationship. Or we rationalize and diminish the importance of the Works S by diverting our energy to other activities; we attend to a different Works S. "I hate my job! It pays the bills, but I can deal with it by immersing myself in my hobbies over the weekend." Not inherently unhelpful, neither are these responses to being Locked In transformative. Getting a new job is an external change, but does it bring lasting relief? Locked In at my former job, I explored getting a new job using my skills in a different industry. But I saw I would soon find myself in the same situation. Like my old boss said, "Same problems, just different people." Change alone would be unfulfilling.

But God's ways are not ours. He works in the spiritual realm first, to produce deep abiding transformation in our core beliefs. This opens us to his power and creativity. Then God leverages the life-changing characteristic of S curves: interconnection. A Jump on one curve affects the other; this induces moves in other parts of our lives. Why is this so powerful? We are now on God's plan, with him at the helm. This is the Old Godly Way! We just have to "ask for it and walk in it"; that is, seek him on our Spiritual S by moving toward him via a Spiritual S Jump.

What brings us to the crossroads? Life! Whether we come voluntarily or it is imposed on us, we end up at the crossroads, and the scripture instructs us to stop and look around before choosing a direction. My close friend Brent knows this full well. He says we're always at a fork in the road. He has experienced numerous health issues throughout his life, most significantly MS. Yet I have never met a more optimistic man, quite remarkable to me. As difficult as it has been, he has chosen to embrace the change, leaning into his relationship with God for strength. He is always helping and encouraging others in their respective battles. Brent is a fighter, and he helps others fight their fights. His challenges have made him powerful in others' lives, thanks to his intimate relationship with God.

We never know when something could happen, putting us at the fork in the road where we need to make a choice. I recently met a 62-year-old woman who suddenly lost her job. She was faced with the choice to fight her dismissal or to embrace the change and move ahead. After a few days, she realized that her former job had been killing her due to restrictions and stress. She chose not to fight and is already feeling a new freedom; she now thinks losing her job has been a blessing. She remains in a difficult financial situation, but she has begun to explore options and is on her way to reinventing her life.

Interestingly, it was an intentional Jump on the Spiritual S (beginning to pray as a couple) that ended up driving the change Sue and I experienced with our move to Oregon. Praying together moved us to Intimacy on our Spiritual S. I am absolutely convinced that this opened us up for our journey. We experienced far more significant growth on both our Spiritual and Works S then we ever would have if we simply moved to the next town over (a change on our Works S alone). By leading with our Spiritual S, our lives were massively and wonderfully transformed. We were never to be the same. This prepared us to confidently consider future Jumps, like my radical career change to financial advisor.

New spiritual disciplines (a Spiritual S Jump) renewed my thinking. I committed to a daily devotional time with journaling, established two strong mentoring relationships, and twice dedicated a day to prayer and fasting. These led to the path on my Works S (a career with a purpose) and were vital support; I don't believe I could have made the transition without them. This huge, scary transition had a lot at stake. I still shake my head in disbelief as I think about the enormity of this change. I never thought it could have gone like it has, but making the Spiritual S Jump engaged God and he showed me the way. I joined him in his work. Who's to say what God might do through you if you lead with the Spiritual S?

My experience has proven that the most meaningful and life-changing accomplishments are preceded by pursuing Intimacy on the Spiritual S—Jumps—with the God who directs our paths. This is the "Old, Godly Way." He then drives movement on the other S curves. Very powerful!

Knowing this, the persistent question remains: Do I want my Works S to lead my life? Well, no, . . . but I have a responsibility to support my family. A really strong motivator! My job could set the direction for my life. But is it worth the price? Does leading with the Spiritual S mean I won't have what I need? Will I have to risk everything? Can I trust God?

> *"And why do you worry about clothes? See how the*
> *flowers of the field grow. They do not labor or spin. Yet I*
> *tell you that not even Solomon in all his splendor was*
> *dressed like one of these. If that is how God clothes the*
> *grass of the field, which is here today and tomorrow is*

thrown into the fire, will he not much more clothe you—
you of little faith? So do not worry, saying, 'What shall we
eat?' or 'What shall we drink?' or 'What shall we wear?'
For the pagans run after all these things, and your
heavenly Father knows that you need them. But seek first
his kingdom and his righteousness, and all these things
will be given to you as well.   Matthew 6:28–33

God says he will take care of us, and you know what? I have come to firmly believe it. I wasn't so sure before my career change. I had to trust him, and all I can say is "Wow!" And I am not alone. I have seen God provide for person after person who pursued him, following a purposeful path embracing their unique giftedness, at times in unbelievable ways. Incredible testimonies! God promises to give you what you need if you fervently seek his kingdom first. Don't forget this truth, but it's not something to dwell on. Leading by making a Jump on your Spiritual S does not necessarily mean a life of poverty, putting everything on the line. All it means is that you choose the Old Godly Way at the crossroads. Don't try to see the end of the road before making your decision. Our imaginations can be dangerous, creating problems we likely will not face. If we allow ourselves, we'll stay Locked In our prisons forever! Is that what you want? Remember, a Jump on the Spiritual S comes with little material cost. Later, when we dig into the Five-Step Process, we'll discuss ways to prepare you for significant Works S Jumps.

Asking myself which curve will lead my life has flipped everything upside down. Now I look beyond the surface at what is going on in my life. Of course I need and want to work, but the questions arise: "What is the right work?" and "Am I focused on the right things in my work?" Now when I am feeling Locked In, I reflect on where I am on my Spiritual S. "Is God is trying to get my attention? Have I grown distant?" "Is he challenging me with something new, daunting but exciting?" Asking these questions has changed my entire perspective and always reminds me of the most important thing: God's ultimate desire for me is found on the Intimacy slope of the Spiritual S. There I discover more about exactly who he made me to be and do. When I can be honest with God and myself about my situation, I come to know him at a deeper level, better appreciate what he has done for me, learn that his promises are true, and lean on his provision and wisdom, the trustworthy foundation Jesus has laid for us to build on.

> *Because of God's grace to me, I have laid the foundation like an expert builder. Now others are building on it. But whoever is building on this foundation must be very careful. For no one can lay any foundation other than the one we already have, Jesus Christ.*
> *Anyone who builds on that foundation may use a variety of materials—gold, silver, jewels, wood, hay, or straw. But on the judgment day, fire will reveal what kind of work each builder has done. The fire will show if a person's work has any value. If the work survives, that builder will receive a reward. But if the work is burned up, the builder will suffer great loss. The builder will be saved, but like someone barely escaping through a wall of flames. The Apostle Paul – 1*

Taking the Old Godly Way with a Jump on your Spiritual S puts you on a lasting foundation. Lead with your Works S, and you risk building on a shaky foundation. A believer may gain eternal life but little else. What will you do? Paul says to be very careful to build on the foundation of Jesus Christ. We are free to make our own decisions. But we should realize that our work will be tested. When we lead with the Spiritual S, we have confidence in what we build. Yes, it will be hard work because the Old Godly Way is the rough path. But it is the one, ironically, that bears the great fruit of a free and fulfilling life. We don't see it immediately, but when we lead with the Spiritual S, we follow the path that leads toward our ultimate desires. Every other path falls short.

> *Unless the Lord builds a house, the work of the builders is wasted. Unless the Lord protects a city, guarding it with sentries will do no good.* King Solomon – Psalm 127:1

When we fail to lead with the Spiritual S, we attempt to build our own little house without God. We build an imposter that won't deliver on its promises. We may work hard and gain a beautiful home, an estate worth a fortune, or a career dedicated to helping others, but it is all hollow without the intimacy with God that comes from letting him build our house. Imagine it: overflowing with beauty, wonderful smells, tastes, warmth, love, fun, joy, peace, calm, . . . Notice what's not there: burdens, worries, tension, anxiety, pain, hurts. . . These things are burned away, surrendered as we draw close to God, cycling through Spiritual S Jumps. Can you imagine life without these? Too good to know! When we decide to Jump on our Spiritual S, we enter the realm of the Lord Jesus Christ, the one with the power, who has paid the price for our freedom, that frees from bondage in all areas of our lives. My experience has been that when I draw near close to God by making a Jump on my Spiritual S that he reveals the next surrender I need to make. He brings it into the light. I must release it to experience true freedom. Jesus is the Master Key that unlocks us from all our burdens. With each surrender I appreciate more the significance of what he did for me. I'm in awe.

The Master Key

"The Spirit of the Lord is upon me, for he has anointed me to bring Good News to the poor. He has sent me to proclaim that captives will be released, that the blind will see, that the oppressed will be set free, and that the time of the Lord's favor has come.   Jesus Christ -- Luke 4:18–19

That first and greatest step of surrender on the Spiritual S, declaring that Jesus is Lord and leader of your life, is the gateway to the Old, Godly Way, the path of ongoing surrender and deep intimacy with God and to freedom. I had no idea what this meant when I accepted Jesus as my savior, and I'm still learning all these years later. It felt good, but I had no notion of the implications. It wasn't an earth-shattering experience, but I was enthusiastic and hungry to learn about God from others. I developed foundational beliefs I could apply to my life as I progressed up the slope of Intimacy on the Spiritual S. In this growth stage we move closer to God, accept new beliefs, and become more like him as we attempt to do what he teaches.

For a lot of people this means following new rules, but I learned that there is much more to it. It wasn't clear at first, but as I learned more about who God is, I realized following Jesus is not about rules. Christians believe in a relational God consisting of the Father, Son (Jesus) and Holy Spirit, one God, comprised of three distinct beings in perfect relationship, a rope of three strands. God wants to share his relationship with us.

Due to man's fall, we are born into a broken world. Tarnished by sin, we cannot enter the presence of God the Father no matter how much good we do—we cannot be good enough. Jesus came to earth, fully God and fully human, on a mission to restore our relationship with him. He chose to become human so he could relate to us and us to him. Jesus is the bridge to connect us to God. Jesus proclaimed that the only way to "know" God the Father (in intimate relationship) is by first having a relationship with the Son.

> *After saying all these things, Jesus looked up to heaven and said, "Father, the hour has come. Glorify your Son so he can give glory back to you. For you have given him authority over everyone. He gives eternal life to each one you have given him. And this is the way to have eternal life—to know you, the only true God, and Jesus Christ, the one you sent to earth. I brought glory to you here on earth by completing the work you gave me to do. Now, Father, bring me into the glory we shared before the world began.*
>
> *"I have revealed you to the ones you gave me from this world. They were always yours. You gave them to me, and they have kept your word. Now they know that everything I have is a gift from you, for I have passed on to them the message you gave me. They accepted it and know that I came from you, and they believe you sent me.*

"My prayer is not for the world, but for those you have given me, because they belong to you. All who are mine belong to you, and you have given them to me, so they bring me glory. Now I am departing from the world; they are staying in this world, but I am coming to you. Holy Father, you have given me your name; now protect them by the power of your name so that they will be united just as we are. Jesus Christ – John 17:1–11*

God wants everything restored to its original beauty, all in perfect, deep intimacy. Christianity is unique in that following Jesus leads to a personal relationship or "oneness" with God, first as a servant, a friend, then as son, and ultimately, as my friend Brad says, as "intimates" (the deepest form of intimacy). This is not to say that we become one or equal with God but that we grow in an ever-deepening intimacy encompassing complete honesty and trust. This differs greatly from obeying religious rules and rituals to become a moral person. It also does not simply point to a servant relationship but to oneness of purpose with the true God who offers deep intimacy and love as only God knows how. Jesus points out that "knowing" God is eternal life, and it is available right now. We don't have to wait for Heaven to experience it.

On the last day, the climax of the festival, Jesus stood and shouted to the crowds, "Anyone who is thirsty may come to me! Anyone who believes in me may come and drink! For the Scriptures declare, 'Rivers of living water will flow from his heart.'" Jesus Christ – John 7:37-38*

Without fully accepting the invitation Jesus offers, you may do good deeds, feel spiritual, refer to spiritual things, even be religious—but you will not grow to intimately "know" the one true God and find what Jesus refers to as "living water," the sustenance of everlasting life. Declaring Jesus as the savior and ruler of your life both with your lips and in your heart births a flourishing relationship; it does not simply mark the time when you began to follow some new rules.

Do you have a flourishing relationship with God?

A proclaimed Christian—either not a true believer (who has never made the commitment to follow Jesus in his heart), or a believer who has become Locked In, slidden backward down the Decline of his Spiritual S and not growing deeper in intimacy with God—may fail to experience this. Someone Locked In might follow traditions, serve, give and do good things, more out of habit or obligation. Those Locked In tend to be comfortable, unwilling to take new and disruptive spiritual steps to grow. This keeps them from reaching a deepening and dependent relationship with God. Unfortunately, this is quite common; it keeps people from living free and fulfilled.

Jesus Christ is the Master Key who unlocks all aspects of your life. I think about it like this: we are bound by many, many chains. Accepting Jesus as savior unlocks the master lock that holds the chains together. We are no longer bound, but we don't realize it so the chains lie on us still. We simply need to move from under them in an ongoing process of surrender as we encounter them. Jesus leads the way, and we grow in Intimacy with God as we go. As we initiate Jumps on our Spiritual S, he shows us what is next for us to surrender, revealing the next chain to be lifted.

In my own journey and many of those I have worked with, I find recurrent themes, indicating our deepest wounds and fears, in the chains we encounter. Fears of financial insecurity and ill health haunt me continually. Each significant surrender I make addresses a different facet of these issues rooted in childhood events. I expect I will continue to confront these issues in different ways in the future. I'm reminded of Paul speaking of the thorn in his flesh.

So to keep me from becoming proud, I was given a thorn in my flesh, a messenger from Satan to torment me and keep me from becoming proud. Three different times I begged the Lord to take it away. Each time he said, "My grace is all you need. My power works best in weakness." So now I am glad to boast about my weaknesses, so that the power of Christ can work through me. That's why I take pleasure in my weaknesses, and in

the insults, hardships, persecutions, and troubles that I
suffer for Christ. For when I am weak, then I am strong.
                    The Apostle Paul – 2 Corinthians 12:7–10

The beautiful truth in this is that our thorns are commonly what bring us close to God. It has been hard to accept, but I have come to think of my thorns as gifts and they have become the foundation of my life ministry. I push myself to face these fears head on. This is when I have seen the strength of God and when he has revealed who he made me to be and what I am to do with my time here on earth. It sure is difficult, but to find freedom there is no way around it. Paul says in Romans 8:

And since we are his children, we are his heirs. In fact,
together with Christ we are heirs of God's glory. But if we
are to share his glory, we must also share his suffering.

To grow on the Spiritual S is to get closer to God; this means knowing him more deeply from all perspectives. We need to better appreciate what Jesus went through: joy, rejection, sorrow, pain, peace, healing, power, love, sacrifice, even death. As we engage the Spiritual S, God leads us to experience and appreciate these things as he knows them. As we encounter them, we are drawn closer to God and ultimately experience the joy that comes from knowing him even amid pain and difficulty, a paradox. James says:

Dear brothers and sisters, when troubles of any kind
come your way, consider it an opportunity for great
joy. For you know that when your faith is tested, your
endurance has a chance to grow. So let it grow, for when
your endurance is fully developed, you will be perfect and
complete, needing nothing.   *James 1:2–4*

Honestly, I've always struggled to grasp this concept. How can this be? It just made no sense to me until I had an experience that gave me a taste of what James was talking about. Interestingly, it was associated with a Spiritual S move.

When I became a financial advisor, I was responsible for the retirement plan for a small college. My company served only a fraction of the employees, but I worked hard, and the business grew. I loved working with the people there. Not long after the key business administrator retired, the new person cut the number of retirement plan providers down to one, and we lost that account. I was angry; I had worked hard to build that group. I loved the people, and they loved me. I felt I was giving them service no one else would. This was my primary source of income. My world had been rocked by an imposed S-curve Jump that hit squarely on my financial fears and pride. My anger turned to resentment, then bitterness, toward the administrator. I just could not let go of it. I worried and stewed on the poisonous "root of bitterness."

Around this same time, I saw a naturopath for a blood test. Alarmed, he sent me immediately to an internal medicine doctor. This was Friday. He too was so alarmed he arranged for me to see a blood specialist on Monday. I immediately jumped on the internet to see what it could mean. Nothing looked good. Sue and I worried all weekend. Saturday morning, while doing my daily devotional, I happened to read a story about King Hezekiah. He was very sick and Isaiah the prophet told him he would die, then left him. Hezekiah fell against the wall and pleaded with God for his life. Right then, Isaiah heard from God and turned around to tell the king he would live another 15 years. Like no other time, I could totally relate to what Hezekiah went through, I felt such a deep groaning from within. I was pleading for my life too. Agonizing! At last Monday came and Sue and I could see the blood specialist. The name of the practice, shown on the building, included "Cancer." That didn't help. I took a deep breath and went in. Time in the waiting room dragged, an eternity. Finally they took a sample of my blood. We waited in the lobby, then in the exam room. Sue was crying, I was trying to stay strong. After another eternity, the doctor came in and said, "Not sure why you are here, everything looks just fine." Unbelievable! A miracle, as far as I'm concerned. Later, I was really struck by the connection with the story of Hezekiah. Why did God share that story right then? Coincidence? I got this peaceful feeling that God "has me." Two days later, as I was praying, God brought my bitterness to a head. I wept as I prayed. I found myself saying, "I don't want to live like this anymore!" When Sue woke up I told her how I felt, my fear of failing. Immediately the bitterness and anger disappeared. A huge burden lifted off and never returned. Through all this, I received a glimpse of the joy James spoke of. Knowing that the God of the universe "has me" is just too good!

Jesus is the Master Key who unlocks our lives. He has broken the chains that bound us. He has come to fill the void in us, that inexplicable emptiness we can't quite fill with anything else, as hard as we try. As you engage the Spiritual S you will be faced with the chains that still lie on you. Ironically, as you seek to be filled he will lead you to what you need to surrender. In this case, I had to surrender my financial life, my pride and fear of rejection. I decided to trust God's promises to provide and not let the fear of man rule my life. The resulting bitterness was literally killing me, I could no longer stay there. God used this situation to bring me to my knees and into deeper intimacy and trust than I had ever had with him before. This was a time of significant growth on my Spiritual S and I learned a fundamental principle: for something new to grow, something must die. This happens with every S-curve Jump. There is no way around it.

From Death Comes Freedom

Jesus replied, "Now the time has come for the Son of Man to enter into his glory. I tell you the truth, unless a kernel of wheat is planted in the soil and dies, it remains alone. But its death will produce many new kernels—a plentiful harvest of new lives. Those who love their life in this world will lose it. Those who care nothing for their life in this world will keep it for eternity. Anyone who wants to serve me must follow me, because my servants must be where I am. And the Father will honor anyone who serves me. Jesus Christ – John 12:23–26*

A woman at my church struggled with her finances for a long time. She had some debt and each month barely got by. Every now and then she made a half-hearted effort to do something different, only to find herself back in the same situation. This had gone on for years. When I met her, she had just begun leading a women's ministry and her spiritual growth was accelerating. Yet her financial problems continued to plague her. She had heard about God's way of managing money but never gave it much thought because so much of it seems "upside down" to what the world teaches. Deep down it was eating at her.

One day I asked her, "How's it going?" She knew I was a financial advisor who taught about God's way of managing money. Honestly, I didn't even know she had financial issues. She told me everything, and that she had been praying and asking God for help. In the end, she yelled, "God, I don't want to live like this anymore!" At that point she experienced a breakthrough and took the steps needed to get her situation flipped around. There is something powerful in these words.

> Some sat in darkness and deepest gloom, imprisoned in iron chains of misery. They rebelled against the words of God, scorning the counsel of the Most High. That is why he broke them with hard labor; they fell, and no one was there to help them. "Lord, help!" they cried in their trouble, and he saved them from their distress. He led them from the darkness and deepest gloom; he snapped their chains. Let them praise the Lord for his great love and for the wonderful things he has done for them. For he broke down their prison gates of bronze; he cut apart their bars of iron. *Psalm 107: 10–16*

"Lord, Help! I don't want to live my life like this anymore!" These are the telltale words of Surrender: you pour out from deep within your soul and give up, relinquishing all rights to whatever you are releasing. I have said these exact words countless times, each time sensing a newfound freedom as God leads me from my deep gloom. It seems like magic, but of course, it is not as simple as uttering the words. I've heard pastors say so many times, "Just surrender it to God." Saying you believe in Jesus does not save you; so also, surrendering is much more than mere words. It is a deep and difficult process. We try, only to realize later that we were somehow still holding on, like driving and letting go of the wheel with our hands but continuing to steer with our legs. I like to say that we must "reach a point of surrender." A soldier in battle will fight on until he sees absolutely no alternative but to surrender, typically only after he's wounded or totally out of options. I held on to my anger to the point of bitterness. It sickened me so much I thought I might literally die. I knew for some time what was bothering me and I wanted to let it go, but I just wouldn't. I didn't let go until I clearly saw what it was doing to me. What a struggle! Are you like this too?

We abhor the thought of giving up; we do not trust that good will come to us if we do. "What will happen to me? This is going to hurt!" Our fears hold us with ferocity; they lock us in. As Jesus says, something must die for something new to grow, as nature attests. This is a fundamental principle of S curves. New product obsoletes old product, new job replaces old job. It is no different as we seek to grow spiritually. New belief replaces old belief as our trust in God's promises grows. A surrender is at its core a painful process, but one which dramatically deepens our relationship with God. He knows what is good for us, and he wants us close to him. Remember, God's ultimate goal is oneness with him. How can this happen with something in the way? He so much wants this that he leads us to this point, because following the pain of surrender new growth occurs, our lives are transformed, and we experience newfound freedom.

As Jesus said, after death, much new fruit is produced. Our testimonies are especially contagious then. An overarching theme of the Psalms is that our testimonies are to be proclaimed wherever we go, even to the kings of the world. This is God's primary means of spreading his gospel. It emanates from our pain as we surrender different parts of our lives. God's ways are far different than ours!

The battles you face will be unique to you based on how you are wired and the nature of your experiences and circumstances. Let's touch on three battlefronts of surrender you may face, the spiritual root of every conflict, and the secret weapon God has given you to win your battle for freedom.

Cuts

An old friend was into boxing. I would stay up late with him on Friday nights watching the fights. Inevitably, one boxer would get a cut under his eye. The other would relentlessly go after that cut until he won. Brutal, yes, but we are in such a fight! Satan is the boxer poking at our cuts. He wants us cowering, on guard against his blows, ineffective and weak. Our fears and insecurities grow to protect our cuts: lies we have long accepted. God allows this, perhaps waiting for us to get fed up with getting battered till we finally cry out, "Lord, Help! I don't want to live like this anymore!" When we do, God heals the cut. Yet we do all sorts of crazy things in attempt to protect our deepest cuts.

Fight or flight? Will you run and hide by not living the way God wants you to live? Much like you might let an injury to your ankle change the way you move, will you change your life around to escape the pain? We'll do everything we can to protect a sore ankle—it hurts when pushed on! So we baby it, ultimately leading to more problems and injuries. It starts small but can end up incapacitating us. Or, will you fight? Pushing forward, driven by your anger, you find that you are creating more damage all around you. Either way, we end up in a crazy cycle that is only broken when we heal the original problem.

Cuts are lies stemming from our belief in something that is not of God. Satan continually irritates them, striving to control us. He's very effective at pushing our buttons. That's all it takes.

Each of us has cuts. We minimize them, but God knows our cuts and wants us free. He wants them resolved sooner not later—so in his wisdom he allows the pain they cause. Not something we relish, pain has a way of moving us. He wants us to come to him (so we can resolve them) where he provides us with the truth to do it. Isn't that what a good father would do?

> *And you will know the truth, and the truth will set you*
> *free."*   John 8:32

God's truth penetrates to the root of the cut; it transforms our thinking, overcoming the lie we have bought into. When we are close to him on the Spiritual S, Jesus affirms the truth of who we are and reminds us of his promises, making the lie stand out like a sore thumb. He shows what we need to release, but we ourselves must let go; he won't do that for us. He gives us the ammunition and challenges us to release the lie and believe the truth. Freedom comes once we embrace the truth and allow our minds to be renewed. The truth kills the lie and new growth blossoms.

The Truth Sets Us Free

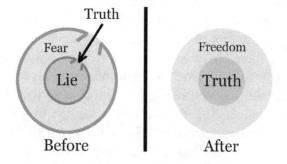

> *Don't copy the behavior and customs of this world, but let*
> *God transform you into a new person by changing the*
> *way you think. Then you will learn to know God's will for*
> *you, which is good and pleasing and perfect.*
>   *The Apostle Paul – Romans 12:2*

If we allow God's truth to penetrate us and we reach the point of surrender to it, God transforms us by forever changing the way we think. He reprograms our minds, giving us totally new thought patterns, and we abandon the well-worn paths we have followed for years. We come to know God and his heart, his "good and pleasing and perfect" will for us. This is too good!

Rooting out a big cut can be quite a challenge. Years of protecting it makes it seem true. We get comfortable with a lie, and our fears magnify until they define us and become a scapegoat. But the truth is powerful and slices through the fear. Healing the cut begins when we identify and replace the lie with truth. What is the source of the truth? The Bible. Healing cuts requires that you have regular intake of scripture and that you are getting the help of others to help you grow deeper in your understanding. This is a vital part of the Five-Step Process.

Life has a way of revealing our cuts. Whether we fight or flee, our behaviors clue us in where to look. We merely step back and observe the behaviors we develop in response to our cuts: our most "Obsessive Passions." I identified my greatest fears by noticing that anything that threatens my work or my financial situation causes me tremendous tension. Losing that group retirement plan early in my career directly threatened my livelihood. What if I couldn't provide for my family? Other advisors I know have undergone similar losses unconcerned. Why am I so sensitive? My childhood memories of growing up in a home with financial problems. My unspoken vow: "I don't want to live poor and struggling!" As a result, I've always worked my tail off, saved and planned to avoid risks. Good things.

But obsession is dangerous. I felt guilty if I even took a day off. Deep down, I had bought into a lie: God won't provide, it's my responsibility. Yet God always has provided, even growing up poor. My focus on that lie produced great fear that ruled me. I've only overcome this cut by confronting it head on, surrendering the lie and accepting the truth that God's promises to provide can be counted on. A life-changing Spiritual S Jump for me. He has provided well throughout my adventures with him. What freedom! And that's not all. Ironically, the intense focus of our Obsessive Passions drives us to become expert in these areas and enriches our lives as we find new strength to help others. Robert Bly says, "Where a man's wound is, that is where his genius will be." So powerful! God brings good from challenging situations if we surrender to him. Your Life Mission will gain direction from your Obsessive Passions, a key from Step 3 of the Five-Step Process.

False Self

Facing your cuts will likely be your primary battlefront of surrender. I suspect that cuts are at the root of all battlefronts; they weave their way into everything we do. Cuts are lavish producers of fear leading to protective reactions, including the tendency to lie to ourselves about who we are. Over time the lies create a False Self who is out of place in the world as compared to who we were created by God to be. Many people survive a lifetime as a False Self. Are you willing to pay the huge price (missing out on living the life you were really meant to live) for this? If not, you will need to battle your False Self.

Personally, I have had to confront some false ideas of myself. Innocently following what good-hearted people told me, financial fears, self-ambition and not recognizing my God-given identity led me to try to be someone I was not. It's not that I was railroaded into following a certain path (though I know this happens), but pressures—e.g., wanting to make a certain amount of money—and circumstances took control. I was also young and naïve. My career started this way. Deciding on a college, I met with a family friend who was a college coach. She helped kids figure out where to go to school. After talking to her for a little bit, she said, "You need to go to Purdue and study engineering!" So I did. I made it through the grueling education and started my work career. Honestly, I'd say I was an tolerable engineer, but not great. Likewise, as manager. Corporate licensing, mergers and acquisitions, the same again. I wanted to be a CEO until it looked improbable. (A blessing in retrospect; I realized I was not made for that role.) Finally, a financial advisor. Perhaps the best fit for me so far, but still not "Great!" Looking back, a common thread points to where I am very good. I believe God has prepared me to be an Advisor/Coach; this is my "Character Identity," the personification of my core role in God's adventure. In the various roles I've had in my career, I have shined brightest when acting as an advisor or coach. Perhaps I had to go through these career steps to realize it, but I think with the right process, I could have gotten here sooner.

God wants each of us to discover our Character Identity: who he made us to be. We shine then in a way that is unique and put off our False Self. God demands honesty.

So engage God and he will affirm your Character Identity. In that role, work seems effortless and time flies. Others notice and affirm you. It's exhilarating! It just comes naturally, because it's the way God wired you. When you act in the role God made for you, your life aligns with the mission God has for you. It's incredibly freeing to cast off your false self and be your true self. You live up to your full potential as he planned for you long ago.

> *For we are God's masterpiece. He has created us anew in*
> *Christ Jesus, so we can do the good things he planned for*
> *us long ago.*   *The Apostle Paul – Ephesians 2:10*

Michelangelo, the master sculptor, said, "I saw the angel in the marble and carved until I set him free." In the same way, who God made you to be is hidden. Working with God and others, you chip away your false self and reveal your Character Identity. A sculptor does not complete the work in one sitting; embrace the idea that you will likewise uncover your Character Identity over time. Think of S-curve Jumps as the chisel bringing you a step closer to uncovering your true self. You'll discover you can do things you never thought possible, perhaps even stumble over others you find you are not designed for. Dealing with your false self is a process. It requires Jumps, honesty, and intimacy with God. We must commit to always studying to know ourselves better. The Uncovering your Character Identity is Step 2 in the Five-Step Process. As you work through the Guidance, you will develop a framework to determine your Character Identity. It's incredibly freeing to know it!

Dominating Worldly Dreams

Dominating worldly dreams also impede fulfillment. Paul David Tripp says that our dreams always disappoint—either we fall short of reaching the dream or we get there and it is not what we thought it would be—but God's dreams for us are far greater than those we have for ourselves. As we dream of good things, they give us hope and motivate us; it's tough to think they will disappoint. Why does God give us the capacity to dream? Without dreams, we have no hope. It's really a matter of what we long for.

A boy in the church's children's ministry I work with loves baseball and is pretty good. Like when I was his age, he's dreamed of life in the major leagues. Last week he told me that after this year's tryouts, he was placed in the same league as last year, while his friends advanced. He was devastated. I tried to encourage him, but his dream was shattered. Of course, only a few reach stardom, but this I'm sure will change his whole perspective on playing. He's at a fork in the road where he must choose whether to dwell on his crushed dream or turn to God and embrace a bigger dream.

God instills in us an inner longing for fathomless intimacy with him. We don't recognize it, so we go seek it in the world. It's easy to create our own worldly dreams, which act as surrogates for those only God can provide. As we progress along the Spiritual S, inevitably we must surrender worldly dreams, whether to be a major league baseball player, a corporate CEO, or to live in your dream house in the country. The good news is that God has a much bigger and better dream for us—intimacy. I think Stephen saw this just before he was stoned by the Jewish leaders:

> But Stephen, full of the Holy Spirit, gazed steadily into heaven and saw the glory of God, and he saw Jesus standing in the place of honor at God's right hand. And he told them, "Look, I see the heavens opened and the Son of Man standing in the place of honor at God's right hand!"
>
> Acts 7:55–56

Amid losing his earthly life, he sees what his soul has always longed for. He's so excited! We get a taste of God's dream for us when we are on the Intimacy slope of the Spiritual S, having given up what we thought we had to have, now relying on God to provide. As hard as surrendering is, if we remember that God's ultimate plan for us—and our innate desire—is good, perhaps we can embrace the process. God loves us and knows what we really need. I can say that though I have released several worldly dreams, God has given me far more wonderful adventures in return. As we surrender our dreams, we give ourselves over to the one who has far greater dreams for us than we can imagine. We have to trust his promises. You will develop a vision of the future as part of Step 5 of the Five-Step Process—very motivating!

The Spiritual Root

Change is inevitable but transformation is not. The natural course of the S curve leads to change—there is no way around it—but transformation only occurs in the spirit. Will you simply allow a superficial change or will you engage God on your Spiritual S and experience a deep life transformation? Change entails doing things differently. A new job engages the Works S and calls for fresh skills and a new environment. This can be novel and exciting. I'm a big proponent of growing in expertise to keep yourself up to date, but if this is the extent of the change and you ignore the surrender on your Spiritual S, you leave God out of the process, reject intimacy with him, and miss out on his direction for your life. Making a change is not surrender. True surrender is a spiritual release leading to life transformation, significantly different!

Imagine a person who goes through a series of job changes to climb the corporate ladder. Very successful in the worldly sense but hollow and lonely at the top. He (or she) has made a lot of changes over the years, but to what end? I know many who have followed this path. Contrast this with Joni Eareckson Tada's story: her choice to engage God following an accident when she was 17 that left her paralyzed has helped transform countless lives of people struggling with loss. She ultimately embraced her injury, surrendered all of the dreams of a normal 17-year-old to God and allowed him to transform her life. I can't even conceive how tough this journey has been for her, but what an impact she has made on so many lives. I can only imagine the intimacy she has with God and the fullness she must feel. She faced her battle and discovered God and what he could do through her.

Meaningful life transformation and overcoming your deepest struggles start as we make surrenders along the Spiritual S. Your battle is spiritual at the root and must be confronted spiritually. Change simply rearranges the furniture, while transformation moves the house onto a new foundation. Surrenders come in all shapes and sizes, all of them difficult at the time, although a challenge for you may be a non-issue to another. But this is your journey, the battle to unlock your life so you can experience freedom and fulfillment. This is the Old Godly Way. As you move along on your Spiritual S you progressively encounter challenges that expose things that must be surrendered so you can deepen intimacy with God. You must face the chains that lie on you. It requires great courage and faith to combat the lies, false ideas, and earthly dreams that have grown from a corrupt root. Alone we are no match for this fight. What makes it hardest, I think, is that we don't know how good it will feel until we get past the surrender. Of course, when we do, we look back and say, "Why didn't I do that sooner!" The lie to overcome is that it will be worse for us. It takes great faith to believe. But this pleases God and he rewards those who do.

And it is impossible to please God without faith. Anyone who wants to come to him must believe that God exists and that he rewards those who sincerely seek him.
Hebrews 11:6

"Why is faith the only way to please God?"

How else can we show him that we believe him? How else can he reveal who he is? We have nothing if we don't believe in him and what he promises. Our faith is revealed by our actions and choices and God becomes real to us by faith. Our faith calls in the power and authority to overcome the corrupt root and win our battle for freedom. It's the only way.

The Battle for Freedom

But when he, the Spirit of truth, comes, he will guide you into all the truth. He will not speak on his own; he will speak only what he hears, and he will tell you what is yet to come. He will glorify me because it is from me that he will receive what he will make known to you. All that belongs to the Father is mine. That is why I said the Spirit will receive from me what he will make known to you."

John 16:13–15

I'm sure you'll agree that we're better off when we do what pleases God. But, if you're like me, you have a pretty good idea of what needs to be surrendered but don't know what to do about it. The lies underlying the cuts, false self-images, or worldly dreams are deeply entrenched, built up so long they have become part of us, our truth, the product of a deeply flawed spiritual root. My issues related to financial provision, for example. Pushing hard to perform at work so I will not experience financial failure is deeply ingrained in me. As I said before, if I take a day off, I feel guilty. I know it's not true or healthy, but my behavior proves I believe it. How do we uproot these lies? Our battlefield is in our minds, truth penetrating our fears to transform our thinking and consequently our root beliefs. Our behavior is a great indicator of what we believe. Will God provide what I need? *Of course!* I tell others. Yet my actions suggest otherwise. My belief is not revealed by what I say but by what I do. To overcome this, the lie must be uprooted by the corresponding truth. But our inner voice repeats the lie over and over, a broken record that must be reprogrammed. So, "I need to spend a lot less time listening to myself and a lot more time talking to myself."

What voice are you listening to?

Lies dominate our minds, but, a new voice enters after our surrender to Christ. What a gift! The voice of the Spirit speaks the truth that dispels the lies and brings us freedom; his voice penetrates the layers of fear and brings the truth to bear on the root lies, rewriting the scripts our lives follow. Transformation happens here, where the Spirit of God comes to purify our beliefs, reset our direction and guide us to follow the Old Godly Way.

Much has been written about the influence of negative and positive self-talk on our beliefs and behaviors. Neuroplasticity is the idea that our brains can be reprogrammed by replacing the negative self-talk with positive. This is not a new concept, as the Bible attests. Notice a key detail in Romans 12:2.

Don't copy the behavior and customs of this world, but let God transform you into a new person by changing the way you think. Then you will learn to know God's will for you, which is good and pleasing and perfect.
The Apostle Paul – Romans 12:2

The significant word is "let." It's amazing how powerful small words can be! We must let God do the work here. It is the voice of God, spoken through his Spirit, that will transform us if we absorb and retain it. I call this "Spirit Talk." We engage the Spirit of the Lord to speak the truth into us. Like all new things, we need to focus, to repeatedly immerse ourselves in that voice so that it's with us when we need it. It is the Spirit of the Lord that transforms the Bible from a book of rules and stories into a living guide. The Spirit dialogs with us in an amazing mix of challenge, encouragement, instruction, perspective and wisdom. He will change the way you think. All you have to do is let him by actively seeking, listening, and pondering with a willing heart. The Spirit is the secret weapon provided by God to win the fight for a free and fulfilling life. Remember, what you focus on increases. We need to focus on the voice of the Spirit.

I have found it incredibly important to foster an environment that allows me to connect with the voice of the Spirit. For me, this starts by dedicating quiet time at the beginning of each day to spend alone with God. I read from the Bible, pray, and journal about my thoughts. This sets the momentum for my day. At the same time, I have found that it's easy to find myself immersed in environments that foster the voice of lies. For example, I realized I was being inundated by all the negative news in the world. I did not want so many of these messages pumped into my thinking, so I cut out most of my news feed. I kept just enough to keep me generally aware of things. This made a huge difference in my life. We are often unaware of the influence things have on us.

Take a step back and think about it, are there environments that you are in that allow the voice of lies to prosper?

Much like growing a plant, we must cultivate our hearts and the environment to foster the voice of the Spirit and pull out the weeds that attempt to steal life from us.

Over the years, I've had the privilege of working with a lot of firefighters. The most significant thing that has struck me about them is that they are constantly training. They train, train, train. Hardly a day goes by when they don't do some amount of training. Why? Because in an emergency there is no time to mess around. They have trained with such intensity they instinctively know what to do, so they just do it. They have programmed themselves to stay calm and do what they need to do. We must train with the same intensity so that when we face situations that stir up our fears, the first thing that pops up is the truth, not the lie. Jesus, when he faced off with Satan after fasting in the desert for 40 days, was tested when he was weakest. He fought back by quoting the scriptures. Satan failed and turned away.

Like Jesus, we must battle lies that plague us with Scriptures that declare the truth. Paul called God's word the sword of the Spirit, a weapon used to defend ourselves. The truth is sharp and cuts like a two-edged sword. Like Jesus, we need to match up the right scriptural truths to Satan's lies. This requires preparation. If we pay attention as we move toward the point of Surrender on the Spiritual S, God points out the lie we are up against. Then we can arm ourselves with the scriptural truth we need.

I find that usually Satan's lies attempt to undermine God's fundamental promises. He wants us to think that God doesn't want you to have what is best for you. One lie that I struggle with is this: "You know you are responsible if you try to do something and it fails." Every time I am rejected I am faced with this lie. My mind quickly goes to "I guess I'm not that good" or "I can't believe it, I needed that sale, now what?" One of my Spirit Talk scriptures to combat this one is:

> "We may throw the dice, but the Lord determines how
> they fall." Proverbs 16:33

It is so comforting to have this truth pop into my mind. I used to stew about rejection for days, now this proverb comes to me almost automatically and I move on. Overcoming lies requires Spirit Talk to be well programmed into your thinking. It begins with identifying the voices in your head and taking them captive.

> We destroy every proud obstacle that keeps people from
> knowing God. We capture their rebellious thoughts and
> teach them to obey Christ.
> The Apostle Paul – 2 Corinthians 10:5

Once captive, we bring them under the authority of Christ and replace the lies with the truth through training. Train, train, train, just like the firefighters! Post your Spirit Talk statements around you where you can see them all the time. Read them out loud to yourself. I like to post things in my car where I can see them every time I get in. Find music that supports them. Play songs so much that they get stuck in your head. Immerse yourself in the truth. Stop a negative thought in its tracks. Sue and I have a saying we first heard from Jim Rohn: "I'm not going to take that class!" whenever we are tempted by a negative thought. This really has helped us. Apply Spirit Talk to the first proud obstacle: Taming the thought that we have no control over what we think. This is a lie. When you gave your life to Jesus, you gained full authority over your body and your thinking. This is powerful!

The closeness of your relationship with God is vital to support and encourage you through the process of transformation.

Surrendering starts with the battle in your mind on the Spiritual S, to replace the lies with the truth, but your Works S holds the trials and harvests, where you are tested. Do you seriously believe the truth? Enough to change what you do? I was faced with leaving my career of 21 years and everything that went along with it; secure work, good financial provision, etc. Scary stuff. The Works S is the field of play, where the game is played; where the rubber hits the road. You need a vibrant relationship with God, strong spiritual disciplines, Spirit Talk and close allies as you make changes on your Works S.

Why?

Because the enemy works to keep you from making the move, or to get you to bail out and go back where you came from. You are at war. All your weapons need to be engaged. You may face times of grief, especially if this is an imposed change. You may be tempted to get angry or to check out. You will hear lots of voices as you stretch forward. Some encourage, some discourage, hitting hard in your most sensitive areas. Be alert always.

Your spiritual foundation is your filter and the source of the resonant voice of truth, the Spirit of the Lord, that keeps you focused and on track. This way you become more intimate with God and get to know him deeply. You see his power and wisdom. You learn what he can do through you. You experience the power of the Spirit. Will you engage the leader of your new life to build on this foundation of truth and take you to victory?

Burn Your Boats

Andy Andrews wrote a great book called *Mastering the 7 Decisions that Determine Personal Success*. He describes seven core decisions that successful people make. To illustrate one of these decisions, The Certain Decision, he describes the story of Hernando Cortez who had in mind to commandeer a vast treasure of gold, jewels, etc. This treasure was so large it was protected by an army. For over 600 years there were many failed attempts to take the treasure. But Cortez was determined. When his band of men arrived on the shores of the Yucatan, they assembled and prepared for their conquest. But many of the men had lost their courage. So, Cortez, in what seemed an insane move, ordered the crew to "burn the boats." Crazy! The message was clear: no turning back. What happened? They fought like there was no tomorrow, and won the treasure. Amazing!

When we give our lives to Christ, both saying with our lips and believing in our hearts, there is no turning back. We now belong to Jesus. The Apostle Paul describes himself as a "slave" to Jesus. We were once slaves to sin, but now we are free. He wrote:

> *"Instead, give yourselves completely to God, for you were dead, but now you have new life. So use your whole body as an instrument to do what is right for the glory of God. Sin is no longer your master, for you no longer live under the requirements of the law. Instead, you live under the freedom of God's grace."*
>
> *The Apostle Paul – Romans 6:13–14*

In our newfound freedom, we have the choice to serve Jesus, and, in response to the gift of eternal life, Paul calls us to use our whole bodies to serve; to be all in. Cortez's crew was all in: they could not turn back. They knew they needed to fight like there was no tomorrow. Jesus asks us to do this same thing.

Do you want to live Locked In, "comfortably discontent"? Or do you really want a free and fulfilling life?

I know these questions well as they have greatly troubled me several times over the course of my life, through each cycle of my S curves, challenged to burn my boats. Would I make the commitment to be all in? Let's dig a little deeper into the story of my Works S Jump to become a financial advisor.

All my Emotional Tensions pointed to me being Locked In my career in the medical industry. I needed out, things were just not right. I was changing, the company was changing. Out of place and incredibly frustrated, what was I supposed to do? I was in prison— stuck cycling round and round, in agony. Secure, yet trapped, I felt as if my brain was literally dying. I had good support from spiritual disciplines, but I wasn't getting any revelations. My friend Brad suggested a day of solitude, praying, fasting and journaling—a real stretch. Willing but apprehensive, I committed and spent a day at a local abbey. Awkward at first, by the end of the day a powerful experience, this solid Spiritual S Jump benefited me long after. Movement began on the Intimacy slope of my Spiritual S. I felt closer to God and clearer about who he made me to be; it was the beginning of understanding my Character Identity.

God had been working on me; he clearly wanted me to do more. The burning question wouldn't leave me: was I burying my talent? This didn't sit well. I wanted to hear "Well done, good and faithful servant." Settling—staying comfortable—felt so wrong to me. In addition, there were things going on at the company that turned me off, pushed me away. (God has a way of working both ends of a situation.) My deepening intimacy with God stirred me to live a more meaningful life. God wanted adventure and Intimacy with him, the Old Godly Way. That Spiritual S Jump—going to the abbey—sparked the inspiration and the courage to make the major Jump on my Works S: becoming a financial advisor with a purpose. This was an incredibly difficult Jump for me, like a person afraid of heights on a cliff preparing to thrust himself to his death. I vividly recall the day I resigned. But I was committed—no turning back—because God had moved my heart. I was all in.

This dramatic career change has proven to be a wonderful place to serve others and stretched my faith incredibly. Never had I experienced God's strength like this before, not even close. My commitment was tested repeatedly, several times tempted to look back. It was hard! But once I committed in my heart to the Jump, I knew I had burned my boats. My life will never be the same, and I have come to know God like I never imagined. I chose the path of adventure. I'm so glad I did. I have gained so much more life. Nothing fills us like the freedom that comes from knowing God.

The Apostle Paul makes it clear:

*"For the Lord is the Spirit, and wherever the Spirit of the
Lord is, there is freedom."*   *2 Corinthians 3:17*

We have so much, yet our souls cry out for more. The reality
is that things of the world cannot compare with closeness with
God. The catch is that we find that closeness with God amid our
challenges: we don't know how to proceed, don't think we have
what it takes, can't rely on what we have, need to release things we
deem important. Freedom and fulfillment require us to accept that
God has designed adventure to help us confront these challenges,
because something must first die before new life grows. By
surrendering the earthly things we rely on and releasing lies we
have come to accept, we experience tremendous transformation
and become contagious. Then we experience a fresh and deep
intimacy with God . . . for a while, only to find that we have started
to grow distant from God and again must jump back on the path of
adventure, once again clinging to God in full dependence. There
are boats to be burned on each cycle, each time God asking you to
be all in, each time finding God honoring your commitment. An
ingenious process designed by our creator.

As crazy as this may seem right now, you will not regret
forging a deep commitment with God, creator of the universe.
You're on your way to the adventure of your life, encountering a
series of ongoing Jumps on your S curves as you pursue the Old
Godly Way. Remember Cortez's victory. How much more valuable
will your treasure be? It's time to put the principles of the S curves
into practice so you can begin to live a free and fulfilling life like no
other. It's time to burn your boats!

Part 2: The Path

The Five Steps
to Unlocking Your Life

*"I know all the things you do, and I have opened a door
for you that no one can close. You have little strength, yet
you obeyed my word and did not deny me.*

Revelation 3:8

God knows our S curves, we don't. So, periodically step back and consider things from His ten-thousand-foot perspective. What do you see? Sense? What's moving? All balled up? What are you frustrated with? What stage of life are you in? What events are coming up? What is changing? Not happening? Growing? Fading away? What Emotional Tensions are you experiencing? Are you stuck? Should there be more to life? Ask big questions.

Recently, what felt like the slow squeezing of earth's tectonic plates—dramatic job changes, both kids planning to marry two months apart—affected my emotions and sense of purpose as a dad, shifting the focus of my parenting. Sue and I asked ourselves, "What's next, after the important responsibility of raising kids?" Moreover, my church leadership role changed due to a merger. Questions were flying around in my head. A long stretch of intense work had tired me out. I needed to take better care of myself as I got older. I felt crushed under the pressure.

Stepping back, I clearly foresaw a significant life transition; not just tired, I faced an imminent S-curve Jump. This comforted me: God had led me out of this spot before. I knew He had again opened a door into a whole new world of adventure. (Each time He does, my trust increases.) Exciting!

Confused about what to do next, I saw hard decisions ahead. I did not want to make selfish decisions, trying to escape down the wrong path, and brush aside the tremendously powerful spiritual growth God had accomplished over the past years. Interestingly, God led me to "Remember," to write out my testimony of how he got me through each time; this gave me courage and opened my eyes to the steps to unlock my life.

A dose of courage helped a lot, but my fears—especially of financial failure—pursued me relentlessly. The good news is that God, as Revelation 3:8 says, knows we have little strength. I am no match for my fears if I fight alone. Yet—what a powerful word!—despite our weakness, God opens a door and shows us the way if we obey. This starts with a lot of trust and one small step of faith.

I would have to surrender something—never a comforting thought. I had faith I would go through the open door, but where was it and what should I do? I knew the tension of the S curve was on me and I would see my emotions swing back and forth. They did, and I made excuses for months before I chose to take Step 1. I'm so glad I did! Immediately the pressure from those "tectonic plates" dissipated. I had moved through the doorway God had opened on the Old Godly Way, made a Jump on my Spiritual S, headed into Intimacy. I heard him whisper, "Hold on!" On my way and fully committed, I was trusting God and his strength with the process. My life opened up in ways beyond my expectations. One time as I was praying it hit me so clearly that I quickly sat up and said, "Whoa, you *are* real!" When you realize God is real, you know that he "has you."

You will experience this too, and it may be hard. You will be torn between embracing a wonderful change or enduring your situation. But remember, the first step costs you very little. He will lead you through the door if you obey him. Start by taking the first small step on the Old Godly Way, a Jump on your Spiritual S.

When Locked In, our natural instinct is to seek solutions on that same curve. (Stuck on my Works S? I need a new job.) But the cost seems too high, so we make excuses why we can't risk it. Or, having lost hope, we stick it out, Locked In with nothing ahead for us but apathy. God may lead you to make costly changes on your Works S, but not as the first step. We must manage our emotional tendencies; we are unprepared to think about such heavy decisions at this point. We can be patient, knowing a decision looms but is not yet upon us.

Smart companies anticipate S Jumps. Obsoleting a profitable product is a hard to do but vital to growth. It is likewise vital for you to identify what to surrender in your life. Go through the steps that follow, and then make the decision. You will need support, advocates to help in hard times. Fundamental questions to answer include: How do I figure out where to go? What is it I am made to do? Where does God fit in? What will lead me toward living a long healthy, fruitful life, experiencing the close intimacy and love of God and others? This is the purpose of the Five-Step Process.

If change is imposed on you, you can move quickly through the steps. If you initiate the change, you may take your time. Either way, don't bypass the not-always-easy process—there is a good chance that you will follow your natural instincts and settle on a change that hinders you from reaching your full potential, the opportunity to transform your life and find intimacy, freedom, and fulfillment with God. Like Cortez and his warriors, your commitment will be tested, but the reward is great.

What follows is the Five-Step Mission Curve Process to unlocking your life. It is best to read through all the steps first so you have a sense for the entire process. Then, go back through the steps one by one while completing the associated exercises in Part 3: Guidance. This is a building process so you should plan to take some time working through it, perhaps several months the first time. Later, when cycling through again as you approach your next Jump, the process will typically be quicker as you build on previous work. Of course, amid an imposed change, you can still effectively go through the process at a faster pace.

Step 1

Jump Your Spiritual S

Therefore, say to the people, 'This is what the Lord of Heaven's Armies says: Return to me, and I will return to you, says the Lord of Heaven's Armies.'   Zechariah 1:3

First and foremost, will you allow your Spiritual S to lead your life? This is such a fundamental question, easy to say but hard to do. It sounds daunting: "What if God asks me to do something I don't want to?" Perhaps you just don't know how to get unstuck.

Leading with your Spiritual S is not hard; it is familiar and natural. Imagine meeting a new girlfriend or boyfriend. You think about him or her all day long. Rearrange your schedule to make top-priority time to be together. Make sure to shower before going out. Once the relationship matures, however, other things intrude. You spend less time. Skip the shower. The bloom fades. Together still, you're in a rut. Smart couples regularly spice up a relationship to keep it fresh.

Leading with your Spiritual S works much the same way. For a Christian, the Spiritual S describes your relationship with Jesus. Draw nearer to God, and he moves closer to you. This is as true for the new believer as for one who has believed for 25 years. God waits for us on the Intimacy slope of the Spiritual S. He wants us to pursue him; he responds in like fashion. But doesn't God pursue me? you might think. Yes! From the beginning God has continued to pursue a relationship.

> *"Surely your goodness and unfailing love will pursue me all of the days of my life"*   King David – Psalm 23:6

God wants deep intimacy with us, but he knows that love is a two-way street. We must also pursue him for love to work.

If you are Locked In on your S curve, it's because you have drifted away from God. This happens gradually. If you're like me, you will drift away despite everything you do: serving, going to church regularly, practicing daily spiritual disciplines, whatever. I tend to fall into a mechanical routine. Oh, I'll pray, read, journal and meditate as I ask God for help with things going on in my life, but I just seem to lose that passionate vulnerability and intimacy with God that I experience when "I really need him!" Perhaps—having not yet developed any solid spiritual disciplines—you have not experienced much closeness with God. Regardless of where we are on the spectrum of spiritual maturity, inevitably we all go through times when we feel distant from God; the S runs its perennial course. To find deep intimacy with God, we "return to God" by taking Step 1: Jump Your Spiritual S. Take a step to refresh your relationship with God.

Above all else, deepening a relationship necessitates spending time together. You may say as I do, "I already spend time with God, praying, reading the Bible..." But is it fresh? Is it "quality time" or just when you have a spare moment? How was it when you first met Jesus? When you prayed so hard as you struggled through a problem? First started daily Bible reading and prayer? Now is it routine? Do you maintain regular spiritual disciplines? Is it time to make this a priority?

You can't lead with the Spiritual S without a strong vibrant relationship with God, as in a new romance. It's crucial. Approach it as fits you, but when the relationship becomes dry, take the initiative to freshen it up. Jesus is willing to meet us wherever we'd like. My friend Jeff connects with God best in nature. When he realized he was Locked In, he began taking weekly hikes. This was the springboard for major positive changes in his spiritual life and subsequently in his work. Others connect best with God while worshiping or doing daily devotionals. Yet others, while serving. It does not matter to God. Whatever form it takes for you, I believe that scripture—the Word of God—is an essential element; when joined by the Holy Spirit, we are opened to hear the voice of the Spirit. Without a scriptural context, nature, worship, nothing will have the substance needed to connect us deeply to God. If Jeff had not pondered scripture while hiking, looking around, or struggling to make it up a steep hill, he would not have drawn closer to God.

A ropes adventure with my church included an activity called the "Leap of Faith": climb a 40-foot telephone pole, stand on top, turn 180°, then leap to catch a trapeze bar hanging a good distance away. For me, this was a real stretch. I'm not much for heights, but I decided to go for it, strapped into a safety harness in case I fell. I climbed the pole just fine, but at the top the game totally changed. I labored to push myself to stand atop the pole. Standing eye to eye with the trees, my legs were shaking like crazy. I never prayed so hard in my life! After a seeming eternity, I got turned around and took the leap. My fingers brushed the trapeze but slipped off. There I was, dangling in my safety harness 30 feet off the ground. I didn't make it. But I learned a deep, deep spiritual lesson. I had read over and over in the Bible how God protects us and is our security, our safety harness. Yet despite my safety harness, I was petrified on that pole! Crazy, yes? I realized I do the same with God. I forget about him and disbelieve his promises. I often worry about a lack of money, for example, but hasn't God promised to provide what I need? I learned a great spiritual lesson at the intersection of this activity and the Word of God. But I only learned the lesson due to time spent in scripture.

So, when you are Locked In and realize that you need to draw closer to God, it's time to engage in fresh spiritual disciplines that deepen your understanding of God's word and help you reflect on who God is. For example: starting or revamping daily Bible study including prayer and journaling, finding a mentor/coach, joining a small group, dedicating a day to study, prayer and fasting, or going on a mission trip. Stir the pot to [re-]establish your disciplines. It's what happens during these times that's important. Locked In we become apathetic, comfortable in discomfort. Most of us dislike change. I get more self-dependent when I'm Locked In. (Things are mostly okay, I don't need to change!) Initiating change at this spot does not cost much, but it is hard. You need to push yourself, but the benefits far outweigh the costs.

Years ago, I used to swim early in the morning at my health club. I'd wake up at 5:00 to be at the pool by 5:30. Lying in my warm bed, thinking about diving into the cool water, the thought of the shock of the pool water was paralyzing! I didn't want to go, but the benefits were worth it. Reluctantly standing at the edge of the pool in my suit, half asleep and already shivering, I forced myself and took the plunge. And you know what? After a lap, I felt warm and awake. Ultimately, I got into great shape!

Being Locked In is one of those times when we simply must push ourselves to act, outside of our comfort zone, to reap the benefits. It's been said, "Act it until you live it." I've had to force myself into new—usually awkward—spaces to grow spiritually. It's no different than jumping into the cool pool water. It's so easy to keep doing the same thing (or nothing), but we need to initiate a Jump on our Spiritual S to dive into new depths spiritually. Like when Sue and I awkwardly prayed together. Or when I spent a day alone with God, praying, fasting, journaling: a stretch for me. I didn't know it—I had no expectations—but these new practices would prove to be powerful and pivotal steps in my journey. Spiritual S Jumps that made me feel uncomfortable and awkward, these highly relational practices brought me closer to God. Then he spoke to me, helping me clarify who he made me to be. This is what initiated each stage of my adventure.

A Jump on your Spiritual S may not come easy, but it has little material cost. No matter on which S curve, a Jump requires a surrender, and on the Spiritual S the cost tends to be emotional, letting go of a false belief or fear, or giving up a dream. Moving closer to God changes what you believe. Sue and I found praying together challenged our beliefs. "Does prayer really work, or is this just a silly exercise?" We had to be vulnerable, risk embarrassment. It required mutual trust. But what we really surrendered was control. We had been trying to be in control, to solve our lack of community by moving nearby. Three weeks later when the proposal to move across the country came, we had no doubt it was God and willingly said yes. Moving to Oregon was the "costlier" Jump that resulted, but it was a much easier decision because we knew God was answering our prayer. God makes low barriers on the Spiritual S and invites us to Jump. Later, because we have already made the Spiritual S Jump, we are prepared to make the bigger, costlier Jump on the Works S. God wants us to initiate the easier Spiritual S Jump, to submit to his control. Releasing old beliefs, accepting new ones. To seek him with our whole heart. That's how we start off.

Notwithstanding we know it will be good for us and cost us little, we often shirk this first step. Satan likes us distant from God, God does not. If we fail to Jump despite his invitations, he might just allow us to experience a bit of a jolt, perhaps a job loss or other significant life event. In the business world, we often said we'd rather obsolete our own product than let a competitor do it for us. It's best to be proactive with Spiritual S Jumps, but if you get jolted, jump in full steam. Initiate a fresh spiritual discipline to move closer to God; you'll need him. Make the move, lead with the Spiritual S. Let God take the reins of your life so you don't waste it. He wants what is best for you and to be glorified in the process.

> *You are my rock and my fortress. For the honor of your name, lead me out of this danger.*
>
> King David – Psalm 31:3

Knowing scripture is essential to create deeper intimacy with God. What are other ways to initiate a Spiritual S Jump and disrupt the old routine? Start doing a self-assessment. Pastor Brad Brucker has written a great book called *Grow*; he includes a simple self-assessment to gauge your spiritual temperature, identify areas you might focus on to grow spiritually, and to set up milestones of deepening maturity, useful for the whole range of believers, new to mature. There is a challenge for everyone. He describes a broad range of steps you can take to move closer to God. The key is for the step you take to make you uncomfortable, something new to break your routine. Just as I had to jump into that chilly pool early in the morning, you too must push the envelope. If it doesn't make you feel awkward and uncomfortable, I'd say pick something else. The cost is low at this point, so take the risk.

The most powerful practices that disrupt my same-old, same-old and reignite my Spiritual S have been: Starting or revamping my **Daily Devotional Time** (scripture reading with prayer and journaling), **Forming a Team** of mentors/coaches, and partaking in **Dedicated Days** of prayer, fasting and journaling. Let's go through each in a little detail.

Daily Devotional Time

When this idea was first presented to me, I didn't really know what to do. I had read bits and pieces of the Bible over the years, but I really didn't know how to study it. Was I supposed to read it through from the beginning? Or randomly pick, reading from wherever I happened to open to? I started this way, but don't feel it was very effective. It wasn't until I happened to get a 1 Year Bible that I really connected with God.[1]

Readings are laid out so each day includes Old Testament, New Testament, Psalms, and Proverbs such that the whole Bible is covered in a year. Simple. This seemingly random format I found very relevant; it was uncanny how throughout the day events affirmed what I read. I still ask God, each day after reading, "What are you trying to tell me?" In his book *Grow*, Brucker provides other good Bible reading and study plans, but regardless which of the many ways you choose, the pivotal thing is to accept that God is telling you something you need to know right now, that what you are reading is relevant for your life, today. It will be, if you are willing to listen. Start asking, "What are you trying to tell me?" while reflecting on what is happening in your life, then pray and journal with this in mind. This is a primary source of scriptural intake—essential!

When I journal, I spend 10–15 minutes writing (in a spiral notebook) what comes to my mind in the form of a letter/prayer to God. I date each entry for later reference. If everybody journaled regularly, the need for psychologists would drop dramatically. It's true; I've worked through many problems dialoging with God on my pad. Something magical happens when you write things down. It focuses and slows your brain. After nearly 15 years, I have a

---

[1] [https://books.google.com/books/about/The_One_Year_Bible.html
?id=v04NAAAACAAJ&source=kp_cover&hl=en]

whole shelf of journals. This vital process connects me with God and provides essential support as I make Works S Jumps.

I spend 30–60 minutes each morning on my daily devotional, before anything else, even get up a little earlier so I don't miss out. A good start sets the tone for my day. Do what works best for you. Schedule time on your calendar, lest things interfere; otherwise, it won't get done. I recommend early—God likes to be first. I'm absolutely convinced that since I took this step in God's direction, my life has never been the same.

Forming a Team

The wise are mightier than the strong, and those with knowledge grow stronger and stronger. So don't go to war without wise guidance; victory depends on having many advisers.　　　　　　　　　　　　　*Proverbs 24:5-6*

When we take a step toward God, we reignite and deepen that relationship. He loves relationship; for that reason, he placed us here with others. I believe that relationship is the fundamental building block of the universe. God did not intend for us to live in isolation. Whether extroverted or introverted, we need others in our lives—the most punishing penalty in prison is solitary confinement. God made us interdependent, each uniquely designed with various strengths and weaknesses, working together to complement each other. We need others to help and to be helped by. Going about life alone is a dangerous proposition; likewise, making significant S-curve Jumps without the support of others is fraught with danger. Victory depends on having many advisors.

On the other hand, allowing just anyone to help is equally dangerous. Even those with good intentions provide guidance based on their own view of the world, influenced by their fears. They will gladly tell you what they would do if they were you, perhaps in convincing words. This is unhelpful and can lead you to remain Locked In, or take you down the wrong path. It is your life, not theirs. Beware of letting just anyone on your team. What you need is just a few who are 100% for you to provide encouragement and godly wisdom, to turn you to God so you can find the path for yourself. It's best if they have experience making Jumps in their own lives. I always liked the old saying, "Too many cooks spoil the broth." Think about what happens in the kitchen at the holidays. One person (Sue, in our house) takes the lead; everyone else must become a sous chef or get out of the kitchen. When making S-curve Jumps, you are the chef. What you do with your life is ultimately between you and God.

Two to four close trusted mentors/coaches, having different backgrounds, experiences and gifts, have been vital over the years in helping me make my S-curve Jumps. You will need to form your own small team to support you in making Jumps. As they get to know you, they affirm who God made you to be, encourage you and give you a place to reflect as you process things. They absolutely need to be a strong Biblical source of wisdom and direction to God. (If they aren't, find someone else.) I try to meet with my team members individually for one hour every two weeks or so; in intense times, more often. You don't necessarily need to formalize your team and label the relationship. Mine have grown based on mutual respect and support. I'm not even sure they all realize they are on my team. The other beautiful thing is that these relationships are two-way streets. I fill and am filled. Before you make a significant S-curve Jump, form your team and commit to meet regularly with each of them. You will need their support for the adventure.

Dedicated Days

My most impactful experiences with God have been when I have dedicated a day to spend with God alone, in seclusion, to study, journal, and pray while fasting. Such a day has preceded each of my major Works S Jumps.

My first time really pushed the envelope. I went to a nearby abbey that offered day rooms with a stack of books, a pen and a pad of paper. I felt very awkward, not knowing what to do or expect. I just sat down in a chair and decided to pray first. Then reading, journaling, even a short nap. I bounced between reading and journaling and reflecting. The fasting brought a deeper focus to everything. Before I knew it, the day was over.

I find that while I always feel some immediate direction and clarity, what hits me later, each time, is the most significant.

This is particularly true the last time I took a Dedicated Day, the time I described earlier as feeling pressure like tectonic plates. I had just happened, at the last minute, to bring along a personal strengths evaluation from years earlier. During the day, I read it through and highlighted some parts. This is when God helped me discover my Character Identity; Advisor/Coach. The way it came about was startling. As the day came to an end, just as I finished praying I heard, "Do it more." Just a simple thought, but it's hung with me ever since. So I began to "Be an Advisor/Coach" and "Do it more." The pressure lifted and I have felt free ever since. Those tectonic-plate-like forces have not gone away, but they no longer weigh on me.

Once again, a Dedicated Day has pivotally impacted my life. It would be easy for you to read this and say it sounds good but never do it—"too mushy!" I can only reiterate that what I have experienced has been incredibly significant. My friend Jeff does it alone in the woods; perhaps that works better for you. Why be afraid of taking time alone with God? If you are serious about unlocking your life, take the chance. What do you have to lose?

You will find that keeping these disciplines fresh is crucial to help you throughout your journey. You need the steadiness of your Daily Devotional, which fills you with scripture and builds a strong foundation of dialog with God that changes as you go.

So then, since we have a great High Priest who has entered heaven, Jesus the Son of God, let us hold firmly to what we believe. This High Priest of ours understands our weaknesses, for he faced all of the same testings we do, yet he did not sin. So let us come boldly to the throne of

*our gracious God. There we will receive his mercy, and we
will find grace to help us when we need it most.*
Hebrews 4:14–16

The wisdom and support of your mentor/coaches will strengthen you.

*A person standing alone can be attacked and defeated,
but two can stand back-to-back and conquer. Three are
even better, for a triple-braided cord is not easily broken.*
Ecclesiastes 4:12

The deep direction received from God during Dedicated Days will set the course for your life, affirm and enable who God made you to be, and give you the courage to be bold.

*The wicked run away when no one is chasing them, but
the godly are as bold as lions.*   Proverbs 28:1

These are not hard steps to take, nor do they cost you much. But they are powerful because they engage the Spiritual S. You move toward God. In return, he moves closer to you, bringing with him his power and wisdom. Practicing spiritual disciplines really is the way you meet with God. They are the means for you to get to the heart of your issues. Your spiritual disciplines foster the environment that enables you to surrender spiritually and support you through the process.

When you are Locked In, you must learn what blocks you from a more intimate relationship with God. Even people with a long-time, vibrant, close walk with God find themselves blocked by something. Often the stakes are bigger the more mature you are. Regardless of your situation, the ball is in your court to surrender spiritually (to Jump on your Spiritual S). Scripture, coupled with the Holy Spirit, will penetrate to reveal to you where your true struggle is; the fears and lies that are keeping you from being all God has you here to be. Fresh, vibrant spiritual disciplines give you the platform for the truth to be heard and to work in you, leading you into deepening intimacy with God.

Step 2

Uncover your Character Identity

"For everything comes from him and exists by his power and is intended for his glory. All glory to him forever! Amen."   *The Apostle Paul – Romans 11:36*

The milieu we live in induces us to describe ourselves by what we do, not who we are. God's way is first about who you are; that leads to what you do. God has made and gifted you with a unique mix of abilities for the purpose of working together with others to bring him glory. Over time, he allows us to experience different things in life (both positive and negative) where we develop skills, character and passions. The world, with all its brokenness, acts to confuse us, leading us to forget about (or not even realize) all that God has made us to be. As you reignite your Spiritual S, God illuminates that identity, where the Spiritual S and Works S interconnect. Most of us have a lot to figure out, because it's so easy to get twisted around, trying to make it in this world. We end up leading with the Works S instead of the Spiritual S. Everything from parents, teachers, and home situations to our worldly desire for things or a certain lifestyle lead us down paths we are unsuited for. I've met doctors who should be inventors and technicians who should be singers.

One woman I met was training to be a nurse when her husband left her. Being a young mom, single and newly divorced, she needed a stable job, so she worked for the state as an administrative assistant and was still there 25 years later. She admitted that she was not a very good administrative assistant and it was a real struggle each day. As we talked, I could see she had a strong gift of mercy, left unused! Her nursing passion was a dream lost in circumstances. She was Locked In and had no idea how to get out. Her eyes welled up with tears as we discussed a possible path for her to Jump an S curve and use her gifts. She had given up on her dream.

Like this woman, we often get by well enough in the wrong role, but we don't thrive; it's burdensome. Our passion, moderate. On the other hand, when I meet those perfectly fit for what they do, wow! It's exciting! It can make you envious. You may find yourself asking, "Could I ever get to do what I really like to do?" Answering this question starts with a clear understanding of who God made you to be. Engaging God on the Spiritual S is to know him better as he helps you know yourself better. God knows you in your truest form: he made you. He knows all about you and intends to use you for his glory.

As we engage the Spiritual S, God leads us to be honest with ourselves, shed misconceptions and embrace our gifts. This has two sides: to admit who we are not (but not overstate it), and to accept and affirm who we are (and not downplay it). Being true to ourselves is liberating and enables us to operate in our "groove," when we fully use our gifts doing what comes to us so quickly and easily. We assume that what comes easy and naturally to us must be easy for others as well. We take our gifts for granted. I recently met an artist who told me she sees color so clearly that it's obvious to her what goes together. She can distinguish subtle shades of white without side-to-side comparison and had always assumed everyone could. To me, it's all just white! It's time to be honest with yourself. To be confident in your strengths. This is not pride, it is trusting that God has gifted you. The Apostle Paul says:

Because of the privilege and authority God has given me, I give each of you this warning: Don't think you are better than you really are. Be honest in your evaluation of yourselves, measuring yourselves by the faith God has given us. The Apostle Paul – Romans 12:3

We are to be honest about our gifting and not understate it. It is not boasting. God wants us to accept and use our gifts boldly.

Discovering your identity is not an overnight revelation. Most of us just have too much baggage hanging on us, and our fears make us cling to our false selves. Even if you have an idea of who you are, it is important to continually engage the world in new ways so that you can learn what you don't yet know about yourself. When we stretch ourselves with adventure, we shed false beliefs and uncover abilities we never knew we had. Clarity comes as we peel away more and more of the chains still lying on us. This intimate process of adventuring with God is not always easy. Like Michelangelo's block of marble, sometimes we need a large chunk removed, other times just a small chip. Will you commit to being open and willing to let the artist do his work? Accepting the truth about who I am and who I am not has been incredibly liberating. Be willing to embrace the outcome yet to come. It's when you act as yourself that you are liberated to live a free and fulfilling life.

When I made the Works S Jump to become a financial advisor, my whole world turned upside down. In my prior career, I worked with the same people all the time, leading teams, solving problems, etc. The work came to me. But as a financial advisor I had to pursue people, to initiate discussions with people I didn't know. Yikes! The thought scared me to death.

I was very shy growing up. Standing in front of my high school English class to present a report, my legs were literally shaking! Making the Jump to become an advisor forced me into a very uncomfortable space. I was committed though, and no turning back. I had burned my boats. It was tough! But in the end connecting with people became quite natural. I even began holding seminars in front of 40–100+ people. No shaking knees. Countless compliments from attendees. Who would have guessed? Without making that Jump, my gift would have lain dormant, nor would I have become all that God had in store. At the same time, without first engaging God on my Spiritual S, I would have been unable to overcome those fears. I had to let go of my insecurities, which brought me way closer to God, and through this, he revealed to me more about who I am.

To become all that God intended, you must Jump. This is how the chains are removed and your true identity shines through. This is how, over time, you unveil the Character Identity that describes the role that God has designed just for you. I can tell you that it's incredible to know God's role for you in his great story.

God will reveal his role for you as you travel along on your adventure making S-curve Jumps when you commit to becoming a curious student of yourself. Make this a primary focus, continually asking God to open your eyes. Notice what comes naturally; where you excel without tiring; where you struggle and get frustrated. Over time, you will notice common threads woven through your life. Develop an ongoing dialog with God, asking him to reveal more to you. Think of when you were young and lost track of time. What were you doing? Did you find yourself hanging around with people all the time, organizing teams? Were you always creating things? Did you get immersed in a subject or bounce from one to another? Were you always building? Did you push the limits or follow the rules? These clues point to your Character Identity. Ask God, "What are you teaching me now?" Listen to what others say about you. What compliments are you receiving? Stand back and observe your life. What do you do differently than others in your same situation? Often it is even more important to admit what you are not.

Be honest; this is just between you and God. Let go of the lies and pretense. This is a surrendering process. Pride may attempt to hold you back but remember: you will be much happier and better suited for what you are going to do than what you are doing now. Such an important vision to hold. I think about the Apostle Paul's description:

> Yes, the body has many different parts, not just one part.
> If the foot says, "I am not a part of the body because I am
> not a hand," that does not make it any less a part of the
> body. And if the ear says, "I am not part of the body
> because I am not an eye," would that make it any less a
> part of the body? If the whole body were an eye, how
> would you hear? Or if your whole body were an ear, how
> would you smell anything? But our bodies have many

*parts, and God has put each part just where he wants it.
How strange a body would be if it had only one part!*
          The Apostle Paul – 1 Corinthians 12:14–19

If we are an ear we must be an ear, and that is significant. We cannot all be eyes. Some parts are to be covered. If you are a quiet and hidden part, it's okay. You are a vital part of the body! God has made each of us unique to make the whole kingdom work as a complete body. We must commit to strip away the lies and move to become who he made us to be. This glorifies God. You want this, right?

I live in Oregon, and Mt. Hood is very prominent. When I first moved to Portland, it took me a while to know what Mt. Hood looked like. Then, we took a trip east and I wondered as I saw Mt. Hood from the other side. It looked so different. Then I climbed it. Totally different! Mt Hood did not change, but my perspective did. Putting it all together I now have a much better understanding of the mountain. Analogously, you will need to get different forms of input as you study yourself to discover your Character Identity. You probably already have a good idea of who you are. Now dig deep, for different perspectives. Personality assessment tools such as CliftonStrengths and Myers-Briggs can be a very beneficial starting point. Answer a series of questions, and these tools produce a description of how you are wired. I've always been surprised with how well the descriptions match my behavior. I still can't comprehend how they come up with these descriptions based on answering a few simple questions—incredible! I encourage you to use several of these tools because they each look at you in a slightly different way.

The results in themselves are informative, but engage God in the process, and he opens things up and gives them meaning. It is valuable, too, to share your results with a coach who can help you reflect and integrate the pieces. Be wary of sharing with just anyone. People look at you through their own eyes, experiences and fears, and unconsciously project limitations on you or tell you what to do. Many of our false views of ourselves come from others, sometimes even those closest to us. Consider others, but lest they inadvertently sabotage you, lean on God; set aside dedicated time alone with him to ponder the results. God has a way of lifting the key pieces to the surface if you let him, and he is incredibly encouraging. He is totally for you.

Focus and build on your strengths. Not that you ignore your weaknesses, but your strengths are what define you, what set you apart from others, and come naturally without excessive effort. As you make S-curve Jumps, strive toward roles that stretch you into new areas while capitalizing on your strengths. For example, if one of your strengths is "Achiever," then push yourself into roles that are challenging, goal oriented, perhaps more entrepreneurial. You'll want to get in a little over your head. Or if one of your strengths is "Includer," then foster opportunities that bring people together, perhaps as a leader or team organizer; move away from a role that is too isolating.

Working through this refining process of introspection, self-analysis, and discovery through stretching S-curve Jumps, you may start to see the solidification of your unique Character Identity. Be patient; it may take quite some time. Years, perhaps. Like actors in a play, we have a role in God's plan, and I think we all intuitively know that it's about playing the right part, that unique role God has designed us for. A casting director with a specific character in mind looks for just the right person to make the play the way he wants it. God has an open character in his play and has designed you to fill it. Personify your character as a role (not an occupation!) to guide you and describe yourself to others. For example, if I identify myself as a teacher, perhaps we have an idea of who I am comes to mind. But if I am a "researcher/teacher" my identification happens on a different plane. Still a teacher, but the additional character descriptor paints a picture of my persona, now casting a different picture of who I am. To capture a gripping image of your character's identity (your Character Identity), put together two roles. Some examples:

- "visionary/builder"
- "creator/teacher"
- "caregiver/encourager"
- "organizer/supporter"

What images do you get from these?

You are on track when, looking back, you see yourself often playing that role. I realized I was an advisor/coach because in each job over my career I spent my time helping others succeed and giving instruction. My mother recognized this when I was young and said, "You always seem to know what to do." Choose roles (not job functions or titles) that embody your Character Identity.

Suppose you are a "teacher/creator." Think of it like this: You work for God and he made you this way so you can't help but take on this role in whatever worldly job you do. So, as you take on the role of parent, you will be a Teacher/Creator in your family, coming up with creative ways to teach your kids. Maybe you also teach art for pay. In this world, we will have countless jobs and roles, but in each of these you will act in your Character Identity. You might say that you work for God and "sub-contract" yourself into worldly jobs. Your Character Identity describes who you are, who you were made to be by and for God. This is his role for you and I believe that you will play this role for the rest of your life, regardless if you work for pay or are retired. You can't retire from God's role for you. I have a client, a nurse, who retired from her job. Years later now, she is still taking care of people. You can take the nurse out of the job, but can't take the nurse out of the person. It's who she is, her Character Identity.

Think of some of the great characters in God's story. What was David's Character Identity? Shepherd/Worshiper? Or Paul? Evangelist/Philosopher, perhaps. Though Luke was trained as a physician, we know him primarily as Historian/Writer. We see God using each of these people uniquely in his plan, whether in an up-front or behind-the-scenes role. How will your role be defined?

Remember to pursue. Every time you find yourself Locked In, wade in, ferret out, and deftly make S-curve Jumps according to your Character Identity. If you don't take risks, in discovering who God made you to be, how else will you find out? What would have happened to David's role if he hadn't gone out to fight Goliath? He took the risk, and approached the fight as a shepherd, comparing killing Goliath to slaying a lion or bear, as he had done before. He stretched himself leveraging his strengths. Certainly, God wants you too to make these discoveries, to come close to him. Whether you are pushed, or proactively Jump, unearth your Character Identity and begin to experience the freedom that comes from knowing and taking on your role in God's great story.

Step 3

Align with Mission

*He said to his disciples, "The harvest is great, but the
workers are few.*   *Jesus Christ – Matthew 9:37*

If we're honest, most of us realize that the question "Why
does God have me here, now?" is always bouncing around in our
heads. Sure, we can suppress it. Only to find it back again, perhaps
after a major life event or time of loss. Surprisingly, I've often
found myself asking this question after a big success. When you
have made a Jump on your Spiritual S and begun the process of
uncovering your Character Identity, this question comes up even
more often. You'll find yourself asking "Why did you make me a
<fill-in-the-blank>, God? What am I supposed to do with this?" We
want an immediate clear answer. That could happen, but don't
expect one. God is more about movement than destination. He
wants us on the slope of Intimacy on our Spiritual S where he
shares some answers with us. Each pass through the cycle as we
grow, we become stronger and more mature in our walk with God.
When we are closest to him we become more capable of serving in
our Character Identity. He wants us ready to use our gifts, because
opportunity abounds, and the enemy does not sit idle.

The Bible paints a clear picture that with the fall of man, the
world fell into enemy hands. We now live in a significantly broken
world, so much so that we have come to accept many things as
normal, though they too are the result of brokenness. Designed in
God's image, we are born the children of Eve. Flawed. Raised in the
brokenness, surrounded by flawed people. When we accept Christ
as Savior, we are born again, in the Spirit, perfect in God's eyes. But
still in our broken world. Behind enemy lines. We are here to learn
how to serve as we ultimately will in Heaven.

Think how God sent Jesus to the world, disguised as a baby. He sent angels to prepare the way, intervening and instructing people what to do before his arrival. Later, the angel Gabriel stepped in, telling Joseph to get Jesus away immediately because King Herod wanted to kill him. Clearly, Jesus was dropped into dangerous territory. Think about it. Quite the amazing Special Forces mission! And why did God do this? Because Jesus was indeed on a special mission (from Luke 4):

> *When he came to the village of Nazareth, his boyhood*
> *home, he went as usual to the synagogue on the Sabbath*
> *and stood up to read the Scriptures. The scroll of Isaiah*
> *the prophet was handed to him. He unrolled the scroll*
> *and found the place where this was written: "The Spirit of*
> *the Lord is upon me, for he has anointed me to bring*
> *Good News to the poor. He has sent me to proclaim that*
> *captives will be released, that the blind will see, that the*
> *oppressed will be set free and that the time of the Lord's*
> *favor has come." He rolled up the scroll, handed it back to*
> *the attendant, and sat down. All eyes in the synagogue*
> *looked at him intently. Then he began to speak to*
> *them. "The Scripture you've just heard has been fulfilled*
> *this very day!"   Jesus Christ – Luke 4:16–21*

Jesus was sent behind enemy lines for a purpose, clearly stated for all to hear. Track Jesus' time throughout his ministry here on earth, and you can see he remained relentlessly focused on his mission. He did not waver, he did not drift. Similarly, God has sent each of us to this place, right now, behind enemy lines, with a certain role to play as part of a great mission. The question is: "What is my mission?" Again, we desire to have God plop the answer into our lap, but it seems it only comes as we start to move. But in what direction? Jesus made it clear that there is abundant opportunity when he said, "The harvest is plentiful." Look around. We are surrounded by opportunity, in every direction. Good to know, since we can't really go wrong, no matter the direction we choose, but staring at all this opportunity is paralyzing and totally overwhelming for most of us. Opportunities in business, in government, to serve people in need (homeless, widows, orphans, prisoners, mothers, fathers, kids, youth, alcoholics) abound. How are we supposed to decide which way to go?

A friend related that a wise man told him when he was just starting his ministry, "It will be more about what it does in you than what you do to help someone else." We are works in progress, growing as we move toward freedom. We are most effective when we lead out of our pain and weakness. Our pain helps us relate to others on a similar journey, and they to us. We know their burden, and it gives us passion and empathy. On the other hand, we have difficulty relating to people facing different battles than we have experienced. A lesbian I know fought, with all her human will-power, to deny her desire for women, but finally caved in. I knew she could only win that battle with the power of Jesus; human strength is no match against such overwhelming forces. She tried to do it all alone. I came away from our conversation with a huge sense of sadness. I felt her pain deeply, but I could only distantly relate. I've had no personal experience nor passion in that area.

> *He comforts us in all our troubles so that we can comfort others. When they are troubled, we will be able to give them the same comfort God has given us.*
> *2 Corinthians 1:5*

God wants you to start moving. What better place to start than where you are right now? Your mission is to reach out to help others find freedom from similar pains you have experienced. What has your battle been? Start moving from there, and God will help you define your mission. Jesus started as a baby, right? About 30 years passed before he announced his mission. Once we start moving, we can be patient and diligently work to define and refine our mission as we go. It's been said that a moving ship is easier to steer. God wants you moving both outwardly and inwardly. Then he will weave the paths together into a purposeful path.

When I was Locked In in the medical device industry, I knew I needed a change. Ultimately, a solid Spiritual S Jump moved me onto the slope of Intimacy. Key in initiating this Spiritual S Jump was a Dedicated Day. Following this, I felt closer to God. Meeting regularly with some trusted friends/mentors (my team), I began to clarify who God made me to be. I didn't know my Character Identity then but I knew my strengths. God had been working on me, raising the thought that he wanted more than me sitting at my secure job; it just felt wrong to me. Questions about next steps arose in my mind. I had no clue what to do. So I started moving outwardly, doing what I have come to call "Poking Around."

Poking Around

We need to know more. I'm convinced that we become paralyzed, wondering what to do, because we don't know much—especially those of us with active imaginations. With very little knowledge of the world we project ideas to complete the picture. We imagine ourselves doing something different and quickly move from thinking about what could be good about a Jump to "what if" scenarios. "What if I fail? What if I run out of money? What will people think? I must be foolish to be thinking about doing this, why am I not satisfied with what I have now?" Our minds are our biggest foe, and comments from others don't help—they project their fears onto us or cast doubts on our abilities. This is the first of many rounds of fights. These forces are key in keeping us Locked In. The feelings of excitement turn into a crazy dream, and it all fades away. We get way too far ahead of ourselves. My experience says this is a time for patience. To simply entertain some ideas. To do a little exploring. All we need is to take a few steps to get more information so we can more accurately imagine. Connect with others in areas of possible interest; take time to investigate, visit people and places to explore and learn. Begin the process of expanding what you know. But don't make a commitment to Jump yet—it's premature.

As for me, I had thought perhaps I just needed to move to another company, a new environment, so I networked with former colleagues, did job searches, sent out resumes, even did a couple interviews. Better informed, I just got the sense I would find myself saying, "Been there, done that." So, I thought, a new industry, perhaps a non-profit. No traction. Nothing but dead ends. I had a buried but strong sense I might want to become a K–12 teacher. I had worked with kids for years. A good fit. I have a strong teaching gift. But despite an engineering degree and MBA, I would need a Masters of Arts in teaching. A radical change. Nevertheless, I talked to teachers, principals, and advisors at a college. Despite my interest, it came to me: I liked the thought of helping guide kid's lives—and I loved kids—I just didn't want to teach 25–30 kids math every day. In retrospect, God was affirming my Character Identity. Classroom management skills and discipline were not strong suits; simply teaching not really a match either. Finally, at a party, a friend floated the idea of financial advisor, God connected me to a manager of an advising firm, I met with him and some other advisors and explored a few other companies. As I played this out in my mind, though a bit scary, such a Jump felt good, matched my strengths and resonated with my deep passion regarding money, one of my Obsessive Passions.

Obsessive Passions

Knowing the direction you should head in is likely closer than you think. It's part of knowing yourself, looking inward over your journey, life events, and circumstances. Our responses to life form Obsessive Passions: responses to hurts, lies, significant life events, or role models. God likes to leverage our pain. I've had a deep passion for money matters, because, growing up, my family faced tough financial times. I vowed long ago that I would never be poor, so I developed a strong work ethic and spent a lot of time planning my finances. No surprise then that I developed a deep understanding of finances, making it a good fit to become a financial advisor. God began to show me how my Obsessive Passion connected with a worldly opportunity which I had begun to understand. I hated to see anyone struggle financially. But for me to be a financial advisor to help with money issues just wasn't enough to make that risky Works S Jump; I needed a bigger reason. During my Daily Devotional time, I came to realize that my commitment to avoid financial struggles had made me a prisoner of sorts to my work. Fear prevented me from considering other opportunities in life, things that I might like to do. I was Locked In! What ultimately gave me the courage to make the move was this: "Helping free people financially so that they can live the life they were meant to live." Exactly what I was preparing to do in my own life and the beginning of defining my Life Mission. First I went through it myself. Planning for and making my own Jump enabled me to relate to people who were Locked In, trying to find a way out. I lived it out as I was leading others! It motivated me and made me very effective. This translated into powerful experiences with people. Intimacy with God made me more intimate with others, allowing me to encourage, connect and lead them on their journey. Thus we bring God glory. I felt fulfilled.

I became an effective financial advisor for people preparing for transition, because I had an Obsessive Passion for managing financial matters, especially at times like that. I knew what I would do if I was in someone else's shoes. I wanted them to experience what I had. My Obsessive Passion answered a fundamental and incredibly important question for me: "Why?" "Why would I do this?" Your "why" is your motivation. Without one, why bother? It is tough to make it through challenges. Without knowing "why," you are ineffective. What is your "why"? Look to your Obsessive Passions to find out.

My most Obsessive Passions have come from trying to avoid my deepest fears, such as the fear of financial struggle. Each of us has deep-seated fears. Think back to the boxer and your cuts. What are you protecting? We develop amazing skills as we attempt to deal with the pain of our cuts. These skills can be very powerful when helping others if we use them properly. I watched my Dad suffer illness after illness starting in his early 60s. One thing after another took him down a notch. I developed a passion—Sue would say an obsession—for health and fitness, because I didn't want to face the same things Dad did. I know a ton about fitness and diet. I could have chosen to become a health coach instead. My mission would then have been "Helping free people from health issues so they can be all they were meant to be." I believe that from God's perspective, I could have pursued either. He simply wanted me to get moving and commit my strengths and ultimately my Character Identity toward helping people in one of my Obsessive Passions, bringing glory to him along the way. My Character Identity is "Advisor/Coach." Regardless of the direction I chose, financial advisor or health coach, it came down to the passionate application of my Character Identity in that direction. This has led me to define and refine my mission.

In the midst of Poking Around and pondering your Obsessive Passions, as you deepen your relationship with God by Intimacy on the Spiritual S, he will lay on your heart what you are to do. This is not an intellectual exercise, it's relational spiritual instruction. I heard someone say once how she envisioned herself standing beside God, looking down at the earth and asking him, "What would you have me do?" This is a powerful way to begin defining your mission. Your Life Mission starts with the application of your Character Identity in your chosen direction. Having been sent, dropped behind enemy lines by God, remember that whatever we do, we do for him. It must bring glory to God by selflessly serving others. Putting it all together, your Life Mission is the result of applying your Character Identity (discerned on your Spiritual S) to serve others (your Works S) in the area of your Obsessive Passions (responses to your pain).

Write Your Life Mission

During my years in corporate strategic planning, mergers and acquisitions, I helped write many company mission statements and saw countless attempts written by other companies. The typical result is formulated by the senior leaders, a paragraph that rambles on, mentioning profitable growth, customers, etc. Once done, it is put on the shelf or wall and not referred to again until the next year's review—not very useful. Dick Barnett, author of **ReIgnite Your Business**, inverted everything for me regarding mission statements: they should be short—typically seven words or less—and capture the essence of what you do. In a business, this concision enables every employee and client to know, rally and support the mission. If a given activity does not, ask, "Why do it?" and discontinue it. This creates power and focus and creativity. The same is true for your Life Mission. God wants you focused. Paul was relentlessly focused on bringing the good news to the Gentiles. Jesus carried out his mission focused and unwavering. Nehemiah remained focused amid many challenges. Their missions were simple and clear to everyone around them and deeply meaningful to themselves. Powerful!

Your mission is most powerful when honed into the simplest, richest form. Remember, a good broth takes time to cook. Write out your mission, for these three main reasons: To be clear about what you are doing (and not doing); to keep on track—important when challenged and facing doubts; and to tell others and engage their support. As you work, you gain deeper insight to what it's all about. It becomes a defining statement that captures the core of who you are and what you do: a short, succinct message with unique, deep meaning to you.

Mission does not come through an intellectual process. As we connect to God, growing on the Spiritual S, he inspires us. It comes in prayer and meditation as we reflect, consider and let our minds run free, perhaps with thoughts about serving others in some way. Keep digging. Ask yourself: Why is this important to me? What is it about my uniqueness that makes me a special fit? Where does my passion for this come from? Listen and mull these thoughts over as you ask God for guidance. Don't rush. Don't expect to get "finished." This is an evolutionary process, clearer as your relationship with God deepens and your Character Identity is uncovered through multiple S Jumps.

Preparing to become a financial advisor (a Jump on my Works S), during one devotional time with God, I thought of the large number of people with financial problems. Clearly an area of need. I realized people's financial lives and spiritual lives were closely connected, side by side. If I helped people financially I might be able to connect with them spiritually and help them that way too. Encourage them to do something more meaningful with their lives. This led me to write my first Life Mission:

"Helping free people financially so that they can live the life they were meant to live."

Later, in the interest of concision I refined it to:

"Freeing people financially so they can be all they were meant to be."

Later, the word "unlock" came to me so I refined it to:

"Unlocking people's lives so they can be all they were meant to be."

This proved significant due to what I took out; it no longer specifically referred to finances, opening the door to help people in areas besides money. Now, over 14 years since I wrote my first mission statement, I have refined it to:

"Unlocking lives, guiding futures."

Capturing the nature of an Advisor/Coach, short, concise, maybe even too generic-sounding to some, it has a deep richness for me. It guides what I do, where I spend my time, how I do things. It has become the core driver of my Works S.

Your Life Mission will be the basis of your life and guide you in making decisions on how you use your time. Not a vision for the future or a goal, it is what you do. The aim is to align with your mission. To drive your life so your time is spent on things that are pertinent and cut out the irrelevant. Whenever you are out and about, doing things and meeting people, your mission, always on top. You are always on mission, dedicated, with ears and eyes open searching for opportunity. The harvest is plentiful!

Dedicate It

*Commit everything you do to the Lord. Trust him, and he
will help you. He will make your innocence radiate like
the dawn, and the justice of your cause will shine like the
noonday sun.*   *King David – Psalm 37:5–6*

Once you have your Life Mission, dedicate it to the Lord and
he will help you. He says to seek first the kingdom of heaven and
all these things will be given you. Each day, wake up and focus
yourself on what it is that you are to do. This is the basis for
perseverance in all circumstances. It brings power, meaning, and
energy. It brings freedom and creativity as you look at life
unconstrained, no longer limited by the strictures of a worldly-
defined role. It frees you from the excuses of limited resources. It
brings life. You align all parts of your life with your mission, first
your passion and energy, then your resources (time and wisdom)
and assets. You structure your life accordingly to support it (jobs
etc.). You align with God's plan, on the ride of your life. Be sure to
tell others your mission. God has a way of bringing others
alongside to support you. You will inspire them, because innately
we all want the answer to "Why am I here, right now?" You will
give them hope.

As you make S-curve Jumps by leading with the Spiritual S,
you find yourself aligning your Works S with who God made you
to be (your Character Identity). You become increasingly more
comfortable with who you are; your Life Mission becomes clearer
and has deeper meaning. By shifting your perspective to be more
like God's, you uncover your true identity and settle in to God's
deepest purpose for you. The more you align your life to this, the
better it will go for you, because your gifts align with your work,
and God is behind it all. It comes easily and naturally and you find
yourself saying, "What else would I do?" You'll want to do this for
the rest of your life.

Step 4

Move to Vision

Your word is a lamp to guide my feet and a light for my path.   *Psalm 119:105*

My daughter, ten at the time, one day asked me if I would run with her through the park. My eight-year old son also wanted to go—music to the ears of an obsessed fitness fanatic! I said, "I'd love to, but I have to finish what I'm doing first." In that next half hour, the kids looked outside and said, "It's dark out, we don't want to go now." I responded, "It may look a little dark, but once we get out there it will be fine. Our eyes will adjust, and we'll be able to see just far enough ahead to know where to go." Sure enough, our eyes adjusted, the streetlights were on, we had a great run, always able to see just far enough ahead so we knew where to go. This has been my experience with making S-curve Jumps. God lights your path to see just far enough ahead. Over time, God's vision for you clarifies and grows into a powerful picture that brings you energy, creativity and purpose. An exciting process!

After tightening your relationship with God with a Spiritual S Jump, unearthing your Character Identity, then focusing on your Life Mission, the next step can feel a little like my kids looking out the window at the darkness. "Where am I supposed to go?" "What am I supposed to do now?" "Do I just drop everything and jump into something new?" Fear of the unknown can paralyze us. My kids ran that night because they trusted me. They had never been down that path before, but I had. I knew the route through the park was paved. We would be fine. They had faith in me, and I went with them, talking to them along the way. It requires faith and a close relationship with God to make a significant S Jump. God knows the path and talks with us along the way. While a Spiritual S Jump is spiritually significant and opens the door for intimacy with God, the physical, financial, and emotional costs are not, so there is little risk. On the other hand, a Works S Jump carries significant risk financially, emotionally, and relationally. With me at their side, my kids enjoyed themselves, learned a great lesson, and gained confidence for the future. Without me, they would never have taken the risk and known the pleasure of an evening run. You are approaching a fork in the road. The good news is that unless the S Jump was imposed on you, you can approach it prepared, already moving and, like running in the night, the vision for you will become clear. You now have a direction, but it's not yet time to Jump. It's time to start walking.

Start Walking

Baseball was central in my life growing up. My friends and I played pretty much any spare minute year-round, weather permitting. We became quite good. Our high school was regularly a contender in the state finals. Our tough flat-topped old coach Fred Heinlen didn't say much, but you knew he knew how to win. He'd been around for a long time. He thought deeply about all sorts of things, teaching us life lessons—baseball wisdom too, of course.

One lesson had double meaning and stuck with me for years. He told us to lead off on second base, not directly on the base line between second and third but behind second base, and, as the pitcher began his wind-up, to start walking toward third. Heinlen's logic? A moving start gave us a better shot to reach home and score with a hit to left field. A moving object (you!) can start faster when moving than from a standstill. In preparing for a Works S Jump, being in motion at the time of the opportunity is key. It's too soon to run, but start walking in the direction you want to go.

I recently experienced this.

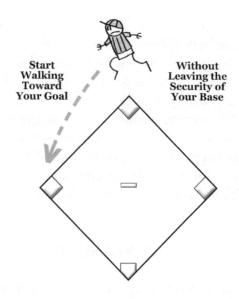

Start Walking Toward Your Goal

Without Leaving the Security of Your Base

The idea came to me to create a two-year financial plan that would potentially allow Sue and me to live okay without significant work income, thereby freeing us to do whatever God might have in store. Honestly, I was mostly feeling selfish, tired, dry in my work; should I do something else, after two more years, maybe? My fear of financial security runs high so, wondering how it would look, I did the financial plan. Remember those Emotional Tensions? I realized where I was on my Works S. My daily spiritual disciplines also felt dry. The thought came: "Go to the abbey for a day of fasting and prayer." I didn't go, but a few months later again I thought, "You need to go to the abbey." This time I told God I would. Finally, another few months later, I went, with no agenda other than to spend time with God. What a pivotal time! (Not that day but since.) God helped me reflect on who he made me to be. That's when my Character Identity as Advisor/Coach came to me; also, the brief message from God, "Do it more." I did: I made specific efforts to coach my advising clients. People commented, "You're a coach!" (That felt weird.) I met a life coach who, after a few meetings to learn what he did, directed me to a life coach who runs a school. I attended a presentation by an executive coaching business. All sorts of things started to happen. I started walking.

Shortly thereafter, a couple major changes happened in my industry that would likely dramatically reduce my income. This was that "hit to left field" in the baseball analogy. Yet I was already moving and ready to run. Who could have foreseen that? This is how God works. Coming close to him, leading with my Spiritual S, God affirmed my Character Identity and gave me the mission to move forward as Advisor/Coach. I started walking, I felt the pieces become fluid, my vision cleared, I was ready to move. Fortunately, I was prepared for the coming Works S Jump because God taught me to Travel Light.

Travel Light

In my vision of standing secure inside the walls of the old fortress, looking out the open gate, the wilderness looked so attractive. I wanted to go explore! An avid backpacker, I knew it's all about weight: the lighter the better, especially when hiking and climbing all day. More weight shifts your balance, keeps you from going places, and increases risk. Who knows what I might run across down that trail? I needed to "Travel Light." This is a crucial factor in an S Jump. Too much weight hinders making the Jump or the agility to go where you need to.

For a soon-to-be financial advisor—especially one wired to avoid financial risk—to "Travel Light" meant to minimize spending and debt, build up savings, to be as flexible and unstressed about money as possible. This was so important; it relieved some of the pressure. Building a business takes time. Many a new advisor, desperate for a sale, quickly comes and goes, because he lacks a cushion. I could approach prospects unforced, and the result? More success! People can sense these things.

When I asked a friend of mine the other day, "If money were no issue, what would you do?" he launched into a tremendous vision of exciting and meaningful things. What would you do? The biggest stumbling block impeding most people from a Works S Jump is financial overcommitment. But is it truly money that holds us back? It is our excuse, often. If pressed, most of us say we believe that God has endless resources and can make anything happen he wants to. If so, is money really the issue? God illustrates this in the Parable of the Talents when the Master (God) responds to the servant to whom he gave one bag of silver:

"Then he ordered, 'Take the money from this servant, and give it to the one with the ten bags of silver. To those who use well what they are given, even more will be given, and they will have an abundance. But from those who do nothing, even what little they have will be taken away.
Matthew 25:28–29

God rewards the faithful by giving them more. It's not about how much you are given initially. The same affirmation and reward was given to both servants even though one started with five bags and the other just two. God is a builder, not a foolish investor. He wants you to start with what you have and be a good steward.

God is also clear that when we borrow money, we are a slave to the lender. Debt keeps you Locked In, a prisoner. I'm always a little shocked when someone is upset because a bank won't lend them money—the bank doesn't think they will get it back; it's a poor risk! Or someone will say, "If I had $10,000, then I could do something, but no one will give me $10,000." No one will give him $10,000, because he hasn't managed what he has well. God works like this. He wants you prepared to make hard choices, choices that are not self-serving. He does not make significant investments in you until he sees you are faithful with what he has given you, whether little or much. Travel Light starts with being a good steward over what God has already given you.

"If you are faithful in little things, you will be faithful in large ones. But if you are dishonest in little things, you won't be honest with greater responsibilities. And if you are untrustworthy about worldly wealth, who will trust you with the true riches of heaven? And if you are not faithful with other people's things, why should you be trusted with things of your own?" *Luke 16:10–12*

From God's point of view, it goes beyond money. Faith, responsibility, honesty, . . . these are the things God looks for in us. God asks us to steward the entirety of our lives. He rewards good stewards with more, because he sees we are responsible.

I have come to realize this is vital because when we are good stewards, we see God at work, make better decisions, and focus on others first. We gain wisdom, build treasures in Heaven and have a closer walk with God, the one who will make sure there is good fruit produced in your upcoming Jump.

"Travel Light" Financial Plan

As you start walking in preparation to make your Works S Jump, this is a time to make a "Travel Light" financial plan, which starts with an honest assessment. Do a complete inventory of where you are, listing out all your debts and non-essential monthly commitments. Track your spending for a couple of months to see where your money really goes. (You might be surprised!) Dinners out or daily coffees can really add up. What can you eliminate? The focus of your financial plan should be to trim fixed commitments (especially debt), nonessential recurring payments, and to build up some financial reserves. This lightens your burden and increases your agility. When I did this before my Jump to become a financial advisor, Sue and I realized that our mortgage payment was just too high. We had way more house than we needed. I realized it set a bad example for my kids for each of them to have their own bathroom. God made some things look frivolous to me, things I just didn't feel right about. We weren't being good stewards. Thus, a major decision Sue and I made in preparation to make my Works S Jump was to downsize our home. A difficult decision, but as our relationship with God deepened, it just felt right. We shaved our monthly mortgage significantly, relieving pressure, and as often happens with a decision like this, multiple non-financial benefits included a solid lesson for my kids.

My experience working with people tells me most don't really know where their money goes. Many have become comfortable with their debt spending even if they are drowning in it. Much gets wasted paying for things thought to make us happy that ultimately fail to deliver. I can't tell you how many I have met who have a monthly payment on a trailer or motor home they never use. Or who "own" a brand-new car but also have substantial credit card debt. Some clients, asked what happens to all their money, said, "We eat it!" Eating out is unbelievably expensive. I can count the times my family went out to eat as a kid on one hand; we cooked at home. The food was better for us, too. A friend, to save for a new home, cut eating out to once a week. She was quite overweight. When she next visited the doctor, her measurements were way improved! He wondered, "What changed?" She wasn't trying to lose weight. We seem to believe that the way we live is the way it has to be and that change will be bad. A huge lie we tell ourselves, and tough to overcome. We are comfortable in our discomfort.

Discipline is good but usually insufficient. Engagement—intimacy—with God on the Spiritual S is so important and supplies the courage to be honest with yourself and make changes. God, who owns everything, likes us to focus on the things important to him. A good steward first focuses on the things the owner wants. He puts first things first. Are you being a good steward? When you are, the owner will reward you.

It may sound crazy, but top on the list of putting first things first, is giving. One of the key drivers to Intimacy on the Spiritual S is giving. There is nothing else quite like it. It's been said you can tell a person's priorities by looking at his checkbook. God makes it quite clear that he expects us to give back to him first. This is not a financial thing, it's about your heart. Becoming engaged with God. It goes back to the Path of the Spiritual S: oneness of purpose with God. When I first started to give, I rationalized it as helping to pay for church costs, like membership in a club. But I have since learned that this is a major engagement point with God.

"Bring all the tithes into the storehouse so there will be enough food in my Temple. If you do," says the Lord of Heaven's Armies, "I will open the windows of heaven for you. I will pour out a blessing so great you won't have

enough room to take it in! Try it! Put me to the test! Your
crops will be abundant, for I will guard them from insects
and disease.] Your grapes will not fall from the vine before
they are ripe," says the Lord of Heaven's Armies. "Then all
nations will call you blessed, for your land will be such a
delight," says the Lord of Heaven's Armies.

Malachi 3:10–12

God says bring the whole tithe. With this, we get the fully
engaged blessing of the Lord. It just takes great faith. When it first
sank in for me, I had started tithing but felt I wanted to give more.
I thought 15% would be good—worrisome for a financially risk-
averse person with a mortgage and pending college educations! At
the beginning of the year, after my income goal was set with my
boss, I started giving at a rate of 15% based on my projected
income for the year. Being on commission, my income varied
month to month. I didn't check on things every month, I just gave
the set amount I had figured out at the beginning of the year.
Come November, I decided to check to see where I stood so I could
adjust. When I calculated the number, it came out to 10%! My
income had risen above my target so much that I was still at 10%. I
was amazed. God works in mysterious ways and we get a glimpse
sometimes. When you tithe with a cheerful heart, you will be
blessed with the leadership of the Holy Spirit, your guide, and you
will really, really need him! You will need the path ahead of you
paved and prepared for you to pass through.

You go before me and follow me. You place your hand of
blessing on my head. Such knowledge is too wonderful for
me, too great for me to understand!   *Psalm 139:5–6*

Imagine life as walking on a trail in the wilderness with God
right there with his hand right on you and working to clear the
path before you and then cleaning up after you pass. This is indeed
too wonderful to know! Think about it. . . . You can see some of the
trail ahead, not too far, but just enough. You are in constant dialog
with God the whole way. From time to time you encounter a river

to cross or a mountain to overcome, and he instructs you how. You need God with you as you make the Jump on your Works S. All the while, you develop an ever-deepening love for Him. As you go, you realize that the less gear you carry, the better, and you know you don't really need it. Travel Light. Think about all the things you carry or pick up over time, items you think you need such as material stuff, debts, hurts, unforgiving hearts, false beliefs. God leads you through the process of dropping all these so you can Travel Light. You don't need them where you are going.

> *Then Jesus said, "Come to me, all of you who are weary*
> *and carry heavy burdens, and I will give you rest. Take my*
> *yoke upon you. Let me teach you, because I am humble*
> *and gentle at heart, and you will find rest for your souls.*
> *For my yoke is easy to bear, and the burden I give you is*
> *light."*   *Matthew 11:28–30*

When you walk with God, your burden is light. You become one with him, not carrying the entire burden yourself.

The other key part of the Travel Light financial plan is to evaluate risks, make contingencies and build reserves. When we venture into unknown territory things may not go exactly as planned. After years of business experience with new products and business ventures, one of my key learnings was that things always take longer than you think to materialize and more money than expected. You have to be prepared for the unexpected.

> *"But don't begin until you count the cost. For who would*
> *begin construction of a building without first calculating*
> *the cost to see if there is enough money to finish it?*
> *Otherwise, you might complete only the foundation*
> *before running out of money, and then everyone would*
> *laugh at you. They would say, 'There's the person who*
> *started that building and couldn't afford to finish it!'*
> *Jesus Christ – Luke 14:28–30*

Consider the costs: think things through financially. Having some financial margin can make a huge difference. People are either overcautious or ready to plunge right ahead. Both extremes are risky. Being too cautious suggests that you are unwilling to trust God, letting fear take over, so you want a huge reserve "just in case." This will keep you right where you are, Locked In.

Farmers who wait for perfect weather never plant. If they watch every cloud, they never harvest.

Ecclesiastes 11:4

Too much caution leads to paralysis. You won't get a harvest. I have often seen people petrified of losing their current lifestyle. What convinces you where you are is better than what could be? Think of the man who has it all materially, big home, cars, boats, savings, etc. yet has a deep emptiness inside. Is it worth it? It goes back to the stewardship question: who are you really serving? Be honest. On the other hand, not considering the risks suggests you are reckless and have not really thought things through. It would be terrible to get part way down the path and have to bail out due to lack of planning.

The place of balance between these extremes depends on the nature of the Jump you are planning. It took me about two years to prepare for making my Jump to become a financial advisor. It was a major Jump! I spoke to a number of people who helped me plan. I restructured my mortgage by downsizing my house. I didn't want that big mortgage hanging over my head. I also did my best to set aside some money that would cushion me if things didn't pan out as I thought. I created a few different scenarios (including a "worst case" scenario) of how things might go, which gave me a sense of how risky this Jump was. I talked everything over with my wife since she is my key partner. All this prepared me and allowed me to make the Jump and not feel desperate for immediate success. This preparation significantly increased my ability to succeed. If planning is not your strength, find an advisor or coach to help you develop a viable Travel Light financial plan. It will be well worth it and enable you to pursue God's vision for you.

Visioning

Now you're moving in the general direction God is leading you, waiting for the opportune time to make your Jump. Having laid out the steps to lighten your load, you are free and agile to let your mind expand on the possibilities of the future. It is time to let your God-given imagination loose to create a vision of the ideal future. God has planted in us a longing for heaven and a sense of what it might be like. We picture ourselves living stress-free on a tropical island, for example. It's fun to imagine life in the sun on the beach. I believe that while there are some good elements in this vision, it falls far short of heaven. Most of us have not spent much time thinking about what it might truly be like. We hold back. "Why bother?" It may feel foreign—and I'm sure that even our greatest imagination will fall short—but a little imagination could transform your life. It provides excitement, motivation, purpose, and spurs incredible creativity. Vision has a way of breaking down obstacles in your thinking. It's well worth it!

Here's a great exercise to help you get started: Imagine that a miracle happened overnight as you slept. When you wake up, you find yourself fully engaged, on your Life Mission, watching it being fulfilled before your eyes. Wow! All around you are people now free from the very pain and struggles that you so passionately have been working to help them with. Your eyes are wide open, in awe. A smile stretches the whole width of your face and a tear forms in your eye. The people are smiling, faces beaming. So many of them! This is unbelievable! What an incredible scene. With the images still fresh in your mind, spend some quality time there letting your mind explore. Notice what is happening in detail. What does it look like? How are people feeling? What is happening in their lives? What is your relationship with them? How do they interact with each other? Now take some time to capture the vision you see in words or images, whatever form works best for you. Capture the essence, don't worry about crafting the perfect sentences; you can refine it later. This is God's vision for you, a picture of what things might look like if everything happened in an ideal way. It will be crucial to carrying you through your pending Jump and bringing deep meaning and joy to your life. Take some time and have fun with this. Some of you may struggle. Sometimes we just need to get ourselves out of the way. If you need some help, ask a coach or trusted friend.

The goal is to crystallize an image of your vision so you can keep it always in front of you. Bring it to a sharper, more concise paragraph or picture so you can grasp it at a glance and think about it. As you focus your thinking on your vision you will be pulled away from where you are, toward the vision. Without it, you will stay where you are. Remember the old saying "What you focus on increases"? This is a time to capitalize on the positive side of this powerful principle. Focus on your vision, and it will draw you like gravity; it will build in size and power. You will be able to share your vision with others, and they will be drawn to it too. Vision is a key element of leadership. Can you think of a successful leader who has no vision? Your vision is a key element that will help you lead your life. You are really following God's vision, and what comes with this? God's strength and power to make it come to reality. Your vision will change your life if you focus on it and trust God to fulfill it.

But there is a danger.

The thief's purpose is to steal and kill and destroy. My purpose is to give them a rich and satisfying life.
Jesus Christ – John 10:10

Satan wants to destroy your vision, to decommission you. You will be tested, constantly challenged and distracted—all attempts to shift your focus away from your vision. The self-doubt will begin right away. The voices will come: "This is all just an exercise in dreaming, there's no way this could happen. My life is so far from this. It's not even worth trying." Satan wastes no time attempting to turn us against ourselves. But Jesus continues to say that his purpose is to give you a rich and satisfying life. Satan is the thief that wants to prevent this, and he will if you let him.

Who will you listen to? I have experienced and seen the result of listening to Jesus. Start learning to trust him on this promise.

Satan does not stop in his pursuit to destroy your vision. Now's the time to build the foundational bedrock using Spirit Talk. You will need this promise and your Character Identity, Life Mission and Vision planted deep within. Keep them visible in your daily life. Post them on your computer, in your car, anywhere you will see them regularly. You want them firmly etched into your mind so you can repeat them to yourself and share them with others at the opportune time. You want them so engrained that people describe you by them. So engrained you will be able to respond to Satan's attempts to derail you when you Jump. As you pray each day, pray for opportunities to fulfill your mission and for God to move you toward your vision. Stay focused and watch how your life starts to move, soon it will be time to Jump!

Here are my Character Identity, Life Mission and Vision:

Character Identity:
Advisor/Coach

Life Mission:
Unlocking lives, guiding futures

Vision:
"I see a growing community of people of all ages that have been freed to live passionate and ever-growing lives. They continue to innovate their lives, growing deeply intimate with God, becoming one in purpose with him. They are gaining a greater and greater understanding of who God made them to be; accepting God's challenge to fully use their spiritual gifts as they pursue his purpose for their lives. They are willing to take the path of adventure at the cost of being comfortable as they courageously pursue their unique Life Mission. They share their testimonies to encourage and support each other's journey. As they lean forward and embrace their freedom, they discover that they are living truly fulfilling lives, way beyond their wildest expectations."

Step 5

Jump Your Works S!

And it is impossible to please God without faith. Anyone who wants to come to him must believe that God exists and that he rewards those who sincerely seek him.

Hebrews 11:6

Everything to this point has focused on movement on your Spiritual S, building a new foundation of belief and thinking. Now in a position of power, poised to make meaningful change in your life, you are well along in the process of transformation which begins on the Spiritual S and is realized by making a change on the Works S. You have a direction and are already walking that way. You are motivated by a strong "Why." You sense God has brought you here; it feels good! But, if you're like me, you are starting to feel tension, a strange combination of both excitement and anxiety. You are approaching the edge of a cliff, ready to dive off and soar, but your eyes are easily distracted, catching a glimpse of the jagged depths of the canyon. You may never feel quite ready, but the time has come to Jump!

I saw a video of a half-dozen people base jumping. They put on a special suit with built-in wings like a flying squirrel, lined up single file and then, one by one, ran full speed and plunged off a huge cliff. Down they went, gradually opening their arms to steer and sail through the air. Absolutely crazy! I'm scared to even be near the edge of a cliff. Though taking incredible risks, they had prepared well; all enjoyed a thrilling ride to a successful landing. I know I will never do this, but I like to imagine I would. I say to myself, "If I knew I would be okay, I would do it!" These jumpers put their faith in their preparation and trust that their suits will function properly. Is that enough? Would you do it?

Like these base jumpers, you have prepared for your pending Jump. It may not be a life and death decision. It certainly will be scary, but there is a major difference in your favor. You know that the God of the universe is there to catch and reward you. The harness that caught me when I did the Leap of Faith ropes course was there for me; it was trustworthy. Now you get to find out that God is there for you and that he is trustworthy. We get to see his power and find out new things he can do through us. Venturing into unknown territory will take great faith; this pleases God. Your relationship with him starts by faith. To please and become more intimate with him, we must live by faith. How else can we come to know him? Remember, God's ultimate desire is for intimacy. We make a Jump, we develop deep intimacy with God, and our life is transformed. Get this firmly planted in your mind. When are you most intimate with God? When you know you can't do it yourself, when you are desperate and must depend on God. I'm convinced God loves it when we're in this situation. He likes us to experience his wisdom and power. We don't like the thought of being desperate, but we find freedom and fulfillment when we are deeply intimate with God. We are most intimate with God when we Jump.

Make a Works S Jump, and you gain incredible testimonies of God in action that embolden your faith and make you more vulnerable, which in turn draws others toward God. We know that, even if nothing goes the way we think it should, God has his hand on us if we are venturing forth in his name, joining him in his work. Preparation is good, but faith in God is essential. You really will experience Intimacy with God, living firmly on the growth slope of the Works S. You have a plan for a great work, developed in communion with God and others; now the rubber hits the road. You have reached the point where you just will not know how it's going to go. Simply trust God, stay focused on your mission and work out your plan. What an incredible time this is, the time to Jump!

It is also a time of opposition.

Vision-Killing Lies

There is a wide-open door for a great work here, although many oppose me.

The Apostle Paul – 1 Corinthians 16:9

The world has been opened to you and you are prepared for a great work. But the enemy is on full alert. Now is a critical time— he wants to brutally stop you. He pulls out all the stops to derail you. He does not want you to make the Jump or a great work to go forward. Remember how Herod chased after Jesus, killing all the children under two years old? You are behind enemy lines, going on the offense. Watch out! His mission is to kill and destroy; he will do whatever he can to take you out.

Like the deception of Adam and Eve, his first tactic is to create doubts, to raise burning questions in your mind. "Is this really worth it? Do I have what it takes? Am I crazy? What will people think? Can I really trust God to provide?" Before making a Works S Jump, my mind races, running down all the what-ifs. The scenarios I dwell on relate to my deepest cuts and insecurities: financial disaster, pride/failure. These doubts seems natural, even healthy at some level—have we thought everything through?—but excessive dwelling on them suggests we are ruled by vision-killing lies that must be put to rest. We cannot ignore or go around them. We must go straight into them. Your Jump will do this.

Satan, knowing your most vulnerable spots, likes to use those closest to you to raise doubts. Unknowingly they become Vision Killers. When I told my friend, an incredibly intelligent and highly educated guy, that I was planning to leave my good, high-paying job to become a financial advisor, he said, "I can't see you being successful as a financial advisor, you're too nice!" In other words, "You don't have what it takes." That hurt. I powered through it though. My boss, when I was resigning, said, "That's sounds nice, I'm sure you'll be back in a year or two." Boom! . . . .and at this point, I had just resigned! Satan has no mercy. You will be hit and hit again as you approach the Jump. Nor will it stop. After quitting my job, the reality started to settle in. The doubts got louder and louder. Doubt can echo in your head for years. They eat away at you if you let them. You are in the midst of the battle. Satan is bringing his armies against your soul. On your own you are no match for him. Now the strength of your Spiritual S is tested. The good news is that God's armies far outnumber his.

> *When the servant of the man of God got up early the next morning and went outside, there were troops, horses, and chariots everywhere. "Oh, sir, what will we do now?" the young man cried to Elisha.*
> *"Don't be afraid!" Elisha told him. "For there are more on our side than on theirs!" Then Elisha prayed, "O Lord, open his eyes and let him see!" The Lord opened the young man's eyes, and when he looked up, he saw that the hillside around Elisha was filled with horses and chariots of fire.* 2 Kings 6:15–17

We cannot imagine the size and strength of God and his army; we just need to open our eyes and see. God wants us focused on the goal, mission and vision. He will deal with the enemy. When Satan attempts to kill our vision by shifting our sights inward, toward our fears and doubts, God says, "Focus on me and what I have asked you to do." We must keep our eyes looking straight ahead:

> *No, dear brothers and sisters, I have not achieved it, but I focus on this one thing: Forgetting the past and looking forward to what lies ahead, I press on to reach the end of the race and receive the heavenly prize for which God, through Christ Jesus, is calling us.*
> *The Apostle Paul – Philippians 3:13–14*

Paul was relentlessly focused on the goal. He did not look back. In fact, it's dangerous to look back. Near my home is a curvy stretch of road with trees on both sides. A lot of squirrels live in these woods. I know, because I see them dead in the road all the time. We can learn a lesson from the squirrels. A squirrel decides to cross the road and ventures forth. Suddenly he is confronted with an oncoming car. What does he do? He freezes for a moment and then attempts to run back to the "safety" of where he came from. I've seen them run back even though they are almost completely across the road. They end up dead! When we run back, we succumb to the taunts of Satan, and we lose. We're robbed of our opportunity to find freedom and fulfillment; a major setback. Thoughts to "go back" entered my mind many times when things got tough in the first year or two as a financial advisor. Sitting in my car in a parking lot with a list of names, calling one by one trying to make appointments was agonizing. I hated it. "What am I doing here!" I thought. But I did it. And I kept doing it. Each day I woke up and focused on my Life Mission. I prayed. I wrote in my journal. I talked with my team each week. They encouraged me and kept me focused. I prayed more. I posted Spirit Talk scriptures on my car dashboard. I immersed myself in God and he pulled me through. When I managed to get a meeting, I was "on mission," focused on helping to free that person up financially to live the life they were meant to live. I spent a lot of time talking with people about what they really wanted to do with their lives. "Doing business" was not my priority. God provided. I still shake my head in disbelief as I think about it. God provided way beyond my wildest expectations. I saw lives changing right in front of me! The fruits of faithfulness in adventure are incredible. I got to know God like I never could have imagined.

You must be relentlessly focused on your Life Mission and have in place the support you need, to persevere. You will be tested! Your daily devotional time and your team will be vital. Surround yourself with Spirit Talk to affirm God's promises and wisdom. Focus on becoming more intimate with God. You will need his wisdom and strength. The time has come to Jump. "Hold on!"

Who's to say?

Jesus looked at them intently and said, "Humanly speaking, it is impossible. But with God everything is possible."   *Jesus Christ – Matthew 19:26*

A couple of years after I became a financial advisor, I was really struggling with a problem. Still new in the business, I had finally started to experience a relatively low but more predictable income. My fears of immediate financial failure had subsided. But I still worried about paying for my kid's college and retirement, all these kinds of things. We were surviving but by no means in cruising mode financially. I still had a lot to do. At the same time, I had become involved in leading our church's fledgling youth ministry. I think because my kids were getting older I slipped in with them. Each week the students would gather and I had to pull together a lesson and activities. It was an important ministry to me but was pressing on my schedule and caused me a lot of tension. A financial advisor's job is never done. You can always do more: follow-up, networking, prospecting. The pressure never lets up, especially in the early stages. Don't press forward, don't get paid. Since I was trying to build my practice, given my obsessiveness about financial security, I was intensely focused on my work. I felt guilty preparing for youth ministry, thinking I should be working. What to do? Here I was, staring straight at another challenge to my trust in God's provision. I was quietly praying and agonizing, trying to figure it out, when a strange thing happened.

One beautiful day, rare that time of year, I had to meet with clients on the Oregon Coast. I always brought my lunch with me (Travel Light!) so after I met with my first client, I decided to have lunch overlooking the ocean. Not familiar with the area, I figured, with the ocean on my right, I would just turn down the first road I came to. A nice covered picnic table at the end of the street looked perfect. Cars were everywhere—no way would I ever find a place to park—but surprisingly, right in front of the picnic table, was one open spot. I drove right in. As I got out of the car, I saw a woman sitting at the table. "Bummer!" I whispered to myself. Now my old shy self would never have said anything, but my new bolder self perked up. "Would it be okay if I shared the table with you?" She agreed, and I sat down. After a brief exchange about the beautiful day, our conversation quickly became very deep. I can't explain how. I told her about my struggle fitting the youth ministry work into my schedule. I said I really could use a full day to prepare for it but was worried about the impact on my work and income. I will never forget what she said: "Who's to say you couldn't work four days a week and make more money?" "That's crazy," I thought. I just nodded and smiled. I asked who she was and what she did (more of my new, bold self). She said, "I help heal people who are sick after the medical community has given up on them." Hmm... She had written a few books. I asked her name, thinking I'd look up her books. She said, "I'm not going to tell you." Immediately my phone rang. I excused myself, stood up and turned around for not even 30 seconds to take the call. When I turned back, she was gone! Honestly, the whole encounter might have taken two minutes. "What was that all about?!" It was too weird. I didn't know what to make of it all. As I drove home, I couldn't shake the encounter. The words "Who's to say?" were riveted in my brain.

My mind gravitated toward a Works S Jump to block out Wednesdays as "God's Day," a day for ministry work. After agonizing over it some more and talking it through with my team, I gave it a shot. What do you think happened? My income went up! And it has continued to increase ever since. Nothing short of amazing. I can't explain the encounter with the woman, but I have come to believe in "Who's to Say?" when God is involved. Humanly speaking, working one day less per week does not make sense, but with God involved, anything is possible. On my own I would never have done it. Now, having experienced it, I believe it.

Trust in the Lord with all your heart; do not depend on your own understanding.   Proverbs 3:5

We can't even imagine what God can do. It is so easy for us to limit him. As humans, the only way we know how to describe anything is to put boundaries around it. We all know what a tree is, defining it by a trunk, branches and leaves. We have states and countries defined by borders. We have Earth, the solar system, a galaxy, each defined by borders, all subject to certain rules and limitations. But who can define God, the one that has created everything? God cannot be put into a box. Not his power, not his wisdom, not his presence, not his grace, not his love. No part of God is limited. So "Who's to Say" what he might do? An intimate relationship with an unbounded God changes everything. The question "What would you do if you won $10 million?" is no longer relevant.

The question becomes this: "What would you do if you had an intimate relationship with the God of the universe, unbounded by any limitations or rules?" The same God who wants you to live a free and fulfilling life, serving him. Think about it.

"Who's to Say" what he can do through and for you? We just have to get out of the way. Those lies you believe and the fears that result from them are stealing your freedom. They have you Locked In. Is that where you want to stay, enduring your prison sentence? Don't you sense there is more in life than this? Look at how God has gifted you. Do you want those talents collecting dust on the shelf? Think about the abilities you haven't yet discovered. Think about those who need your help—now!

> *Jesus replied, "'You must love the Lord your God with all your heart, all your soul, and all your mind.' This is the first and greatest commandment. A second is equally important: 'Love your neighbor as yourself.' The entire law and all the demands of the prophets are based on these two commandments."*   Matthew 22:37–40

Jesus clarifies the most important commandments. The Spiritual S points to the first command. First you must love the Lord your God with your whole heart, soul, and mind. God wants every part of you in intimate communion with him. This is a relationship of love, and God has an endless supply. Will you go to meet him by initiating Jumps on your Spiritual S? Are you willing to surrender those fears and expose the lies about who God is and what he can do? Are you willing to accept his love and love him back? This is the key to experiencing an increasingly deepening Intimate relationship with the God of the universe. This is where he shows himself to you and helps you see yourself. Your soul craves this, whether you realize it or not. Remember, where the Spirit of the Lord is, there is freedom. The Spiritual S shows you where you are and points to the path of oneness of purpose with the God of the universe.

Then, he asks you to love your neighbor. This points to the Works S. How can you use your talents and Obsessive Passions to serve others as an act of love? Don't you want others to experience the freedom you have now? What could be better and more fulfilling than to see others released from the same chains that you know so well? Those chains have uniquely qualified you to connect others with the God who has freed you. Who's to Say what God may do?

God tells us that love is the centerpiece of his story. If relationship is the building block of the universe, love is the glue. He loves us so much that he sent his son Jesus to save us and restore relationship. This was his initiative in response to our failure. He asks us to receive it and come to him. It's our initiative to move closer to him now. He welcomes us, because he desires intimacy so much. He's been where we are. James tells us to look carefully.

> *But if you look carefully into the perfect law that sets you free, and if you do what it says and don't forget what you heard, then God will bless you for doing it.*
>
> *James 1:25*

Being perfect, God has chosen love as the law that brings everything together. It is the power of love that sets you free. We find this love when we do what do what God says: Love him and love others with everything you have. Freedom comes with obedience to this law. Who's to Say what the God of the universe will do for you if you love him? Everything is at his disposal.

Take delight in the Lord, and he will give you your heart's desires.   *King David – Psalm 37:4*

Don't deny those deep longings in your heart. God placed these in you in the beginning. If you delight in the Lord, he will gladly give you what you long for. Sound too good to be true? You will not find out until you venture forth and take that first small step toward him.

Part 3: Guidance

Exercises

... I have come that they may have life, and have it to the full.   *Jesus Christ – John 10:10*

These exercises are designed to help you work through the Five-Step Process to unlock your life so you can live in the fullness Jesus came to make available to you. I encourage you to let God lead you through this process. Who's to Say what he may do in your life?! You have so much to gain.

The exercises are structured to help you establish and build strong foundational disciplines to enhance your relationship with God and others. In Step 1, you will develop greater intimacy with God by starting or refreshing your spiritual disciplines. Consider these your "regular meeting times" with God. Don't minimize the importance of developing a Daily Devotional time, at least two Mentor/Coach relationships, and engaging in strategically timed Dedicated Days. These disciplines are powerful. You will need the support they provide throughout the entire Five-Step Process and beyond as you continue to grow through future S Jumps.

Enter into your times of Intimacy with God with a spirit of honesty and openness. Take time to wonder, dream, and just have some fun. Let your guard down, to allow the Holy Spirit to reshape your thinking. Why not trust God? He has good things planned for you beyond your wildest dreams!

Make it your goal to cultivate "fertile soil" in your mind. Imagine a loose, rich, nourishing environment where you receive great encouragement; a place to grow and foster creativity. After a while, you will begin to crave this time with God. I find that if something interferes with my meeting times with him my life feels off. Pursue him, knowing that he will pull you in and embrace you. Be curious and let your mind explore as you get to know your creator, who can be very gentle but also direct and blunt at times. Sense the depth of his wisdom and the steadfastness of his still soft voice. Notice things. Pay attention to "coincidences" and visions and reflect on these during your devotional time. Could there be something important in them? Ask God about who you are; what crazy things did he have in mind by making you the way he did? Ask him questions like, "How can my hard experiences become an opportunity?" or "What next step should I take?" or "Is there anyone you want to lay on my heart?" or "Is there something I'm lying to myself about?" Be vulnerable with God. He already knows everything about you; he wants you to show him your willingness to be authentic.

During these times of intimacy, God directs you to confront your fears by embracing the truth against the underlying lies, false self, and dominating worldly dreams that are preventing you from moving forward. You will tend to avoid this due to the fear it will be painful and require humility. Overcome this by flipping things upside down. Adopt an attitude of willingness to face your fears head-on. God will be right there, walking with you. He will not let you fall; he knows that your path to freedom requires that your fears ae put to rest. Remember, something always must first die for there to be new life. There is no other way. Lean in. Utilize Spirit Talk to change the way you think, aligning your beliefs with God's truth, to reinforce God's fundamental promises of unconditional love, eternal life, and provision, that he has designed you for good works, and that he works all things for good for those who love him.... God has made many, many trustworthy promises!

The activities for each step include Reflective Exercises to release and encourage your thinking as you reach for God's truth. Then you will be prompted to form Spirit Talk to help embed these truths in your mind. The exercises are followed by Coach's Guidance. which lays out how to move forward to the next step. To get the most out of this process, I suggest that you re-read the description for each Step of the process described in Part 2: The Path before you complete the corresponding Exercises. You will see a much greater impact if you take time alone to complete the Reflective Exercises, writing out your responses. After completing these, I encourage you to discuss what you have learned with your mentors and other people close to you. Don't rush the process; this is not a race to completion. You will need time to get your foundational disciplines in place and begin to build momentum, so I have included suggested timeframes for each step as part of Coach's Guidance. If your situation is more urgent, don't skip steps, but you can shorten the time in each step.

Each exercise is intended to lead you into a deepening dialog with God during your times of intimacy with him. Complete the exercises in communion with him, letting the Holy Spirit be your guide. If you feel a leading by the Spirit, follow him. Perhaps he prompts you to take a Dedicated Day, to seek additional support, or perhaps he brings a new person into your life. I have found that some people, depending on their strengths, will greatly benefit by engaging a coach to help them through the process. You may also consider forming a small group of 3–5 people so you can work through the process together, discussing the results from your exercises. (Be sure to complete the exercises on your own first, of course.) Keep in mind that, although the help of others can be beneficial, the Holy Spirit is your ultimate guide. Embrace the opportunity to grow closer to God. Make this your top priority; it's what God himself wants for you and Who's to Say what he might do with your life? It's time to start moving forward.

Step 1 – Exercises
Jump Your Spiritual S

Reflection Exercises

1. Read John 14:15–29 and 17:20–23. Underline all references of Jesus speaking in terms of Intimacy.

    a. Why do you think Jesus chose to say these things so close to his betrayal? How is this significant for you?

    b. What images do his words "in you/in me" create for you? How might you change your life, knowing this captures God's greatest desire in a relationship with you?

    c. What did Jesus say is the binder in his relationships? What can you do to deepen your level of Intimacy with him?

    d. What special gift does Jesus give to those who move toward him in Intimacy? How is this different from the gift that the world offers us? Imagine: How might your life change if you fully accepted his gift? Pray to accept this life.

2. Reflect on your past with a focus on the S-curve concepts. Write your testimony to remember how God has been involved with your life up to this point. Describe your level of Intimacy with God and sense of freedom prior to and just after times of surrender—which of God's promises were affirmed? Include thoughts on how your life might change if you make Intimacy with God a focus going forward, knowing you can trust his promises. Share it with someone close to you.

3. Based on the above exercises, write out 1–2 short Spirit Talk phrases that capture God's promises and post them where you can see them regularly.

Coach's Guidance

1. Commit to a fresh Daily Devotional time. Make it a priority by actually booking an appointment on your calendar for at least 5 days/week as part of your regular work day schedule. Begin a daily "Read the Bible in 1 Year" plan followed by a time of prayer and journaling for 15 minutes each day. Ask yourself:

   a. "What are you saying to me through this, God?"

   b. "How is this relevant for my life right now?"

   c. "Do my actions indicate that I believe what you are saying?" If not, pray for a change in yourself.

2. Identify and begin meeting with your first Mentor or Coach twice a month. Start by sharing your testimony, your Emotional Tensions, discussing where you feel you are on your S curves and anything that might be preventing you from moving closer to God.

Move to Exercise 2 after practicing 4 weeks.

Step 2 – Exercises
Uncover Your Character Identity

Reflection Exercises

1. Read Psalm 139, written by David.

    a. Form a description that captures the view of how God (the Creator) sees and watches over David (his creation). How does this apply to you?

    b. What does David say about God's workmanship in creating him? Describe what you say to yourself about how God created you. Consider this: If God thinks so highly of you that he wants to be with you always, shouldn't you think just as highly of yourself?

2. Read Galatians 5:13.

    a. What experiences over your life have you had that have given you the opportunity to shine distinctively while helping others?

    b. What 5 unique abilities made you shine in these situations?

    c. Which of these have you displayed in all your various roles and situations throughout your life?

3. Read 1 Samuel 16: 1–13, Acts 13:22 and Matthew 22:34–40.

    a. How was David selected to be king? What made him stand out from his brothers?

b. How might others describe your heart? How does your heart distinguish you from others in the world? How might your life change if you love your neighbor with all your heart? What can you begin doing now to let others see your heart as you serve them?

4. Based on the above exercises and/or your Daily Devotional readings, write out 1–2 short Spirit Talk phrases that capture God's promises and post them where you can see them regularly.

Coach's Guidance

1. Expand how well you know yourself by taking the CliftonStrengths evaluation (https://www.gallupstrengths center.com). Study to gain a deep understanding of the themes of your top 5 Strengths and confirm with others. How do these strengths help explain where you have succeeded (or not) in life?

2. Plan a Dedicated Day to seek God's wisdom:

    a. Combine the results from your CliftonStrengths evaluation and the Reflection Exercises to form an overall unique character description of yourself.

    b. Considering your current work, on a scale to 1 (least) – 10 (most often), how often are you able to express your unique character? What could you do to move up the scale one level? Take action to do this.

    c. Pray for God to reveal: What Lie, False Self or Worldly Dream must be released so you can be free to express your unique character more often? Identify a promise or truth from God that directly confronts this. Add this to your Spirit Talk.

3. Advanced Exercise (*best done with a coach*): Review the Personal Strength Insights from your CliftonStrengths results, highlighting 10–15 words or short phrases that you feel capture yourself particularly well. On a piece of paper, write the words/phrases around the page creating 3–5 loose clusters of similar characteristics. Looking over the clusters, attempt to identify two Character Identities (see Appendix 1 for a list of sample character Identities) that personify the essence of these clusters by asking "Who exhibits these traits?" Examples:

   o Builder/Visionary
   o Researcher/Persuader
   o Caregiver/Encourager
   o Teacher/Motivator
   o Analyst/Problem Solver
   o Organizer/Leader

   Test it: Search for a common thread with you acting in the role of your Character Identity throughout the various roles you have had over the course of your life.

4. Begin meeting with your second Mentor twice a month. Review your discoveries with both mentors.

Move to Exercise 3 after 4 weeks.

Step 3 – Exercises
Align with Mission

Reflection Exercises

1. Read Matthew and Luke chapters 1 and 2 with a focus on the role of the angels. How would you describe what is happening in military terms? Consider your life in the context of what is happening in the world around you. What is going on that gives you the sense that you, like Jesus, have been sent behind enemy lines for a reason? What group of people sits heavy on your heart? Why? How might knowing this reshape your priorities?

2. Read Luke 4:16–21, Luke 3:1–6 and Ephesians 3:1–10. Describe why Jesus, John the Baptist and Paul each were sent here, in a few words.

3. Read John 14:12–14 and John 17:18. Reflect on all the works Jesus did. What is he asking of you? Knowing that Jesus has sent you, how might you make a difference in the world by serving those people heavy on your heart? You may think your life is too insignificant to make a difference, but what instruction does Jesus give to bring you success?

4. Read John 4:1–15. Jesus contrasts water from the well and "living water," what does this suggest about where you are to go to find lasting fulfillment in your lives? Where have you been looking to find fulfillment in your life and has it provided lasting satisfaction (be honest)? Think of a time when you helped someone else, describe how satisfying this was for you. What feelings do you still have as you reflect on this?

5. Based on the above exercises and/or your Daily Devotional readings, write out 1–2 short Spirit Talk phrases that capture God's promises and post them where you can see them regularly.

Coach's Guidance

1. Alone, in a quiet place, keeping your top 5 Strengths (and Character Identity if available) in mind, imagine that you are standing with God looking at the earth. You ask him, "What would you have me do?" What do you think he would say? (Push away voices that say, "You could never do that because...," by telling yourself "But what if that was not the case, then what?" Don't force an immediate answer. Make the following lists as you think this through.

   a. Obsessive Passions: what behaviors do you do you see yourself doing obsessively in response to your greatest fears?

   b. Painful or positive circumstances that have deeply shaped your life.

   c. Problems in the world that seem to touch your heart more than others.

   Review your lists and begin to dig deeper to find your root motivation by repeatedly asking "Why" questions like these:

   d. Why is this important to me?

   e. Where is this passion coming from?

Pray and continue to ask for God to place 1–2 possible areas of passion for your mission on your heart.

2. Begin to "Poke Around":

   a. Create a list of 3–5 people who work in fields related to your possible areas of passion. Arrange to meet with them to explore. What do they do? What do/don't they like about it? Why they do it? What possibilities are there for someone with your strengths? Learn as much as you can.

   b. Imagine yourself successfully serving in each area. What feelings and thoughts come to mind?

   c. Pray and ask God to help you choose your passion area. (Remember, there is opportunity in all directions; there is no right or wrong choice.)

2. After completing the above exercises, it's time to make a draft of your Life Mission. Your mission is the application of your Strengths/Character Identity in the direction of your chosen passion area. Both should be clearer now. Start by writing a sentence or two that captures ideas that come your mind as you answer these questions:

   a. Who are you serving?

   b. What are you helping them do?

   c. What happens in their lives as the result of your help?

3. Attempt to distill it down to its essence with a goal of seven words or less. Remember this is an evolutionary process, be patient, not perfect. Allow it to become deeply meaningful for you.

4. Talk through your area of passion and Life Mission with your mentors. (Be cautious because mentors are human and can infuse opinions and project their personal doubts and fears onto us. This process should move you toward God. Remember, the Holy Spirit is your ultimate guide.)

5. Read Psalm 37:5–6.

a. Finalize your Mission by committing your cause to the Lord and by building it into your life. Lock it into your memory. Post it where you will see it most. Memorize it so that you can tell others what it is when they ask you "What do you do?"

b. Each morning, when you wake up, remind yourself that you are alive today to fulfill your Life Mission.

c. As you do things throughout the day, ask yourself, **"What does this have to do with my mission?"** Then begin to question why you are doing things that have nothing to do with it.

d. At the end of the day, reflect on times during on the day when you succeeded at doing your mission.

e. During your Daily Devotional time, ask God to help you to align your life with your mission.

Move to Exercise 4 after 4–6 weeks.

Step 4 – Exercises
Move to Vision

Reflection Exercises

1. Read Hebrews 12:1–4, Matthew 6:25–34 and 25:25–28

    a. Review your life as if you are a backpacker preparing for a long journey, not wanting to carry any extra weight. Make a list of burdens (financial, emotional) you are currently carrying that will hinder your agility as you move ahead. What keeps you from releasing these? Pray. What steps might you consider to begin the process of letting them go? Take some time to imagine what you will feel like having released them. Capture this vision God has for you in writing or an image.

    b. What lessons can you learn from how Jesus pursued his mission? What made him willing to endure such hostility? What did Jesus focus on first? How would your life change if you focused on this first, too?

    c. Create an image or description of what you might feel like sitting in a place of honor beside God's throne. What words would you like to hear from God when you enter heaven?

2. Read Isaiah 55:8–9, Proverbs 3:5–10, Matthew 6:24 and Malachi 3:6–12

a. Think of a time in your life when you had to let go of one thing to grab another. Describe how you felt before, during and after. What gave you the courage to let go?

b. Imagine you are a trapeze artist and preparing to let go. List five vital characteristics that you would want present in the person catching you. Which of these characteristics does God possess?

c. Have you fully released your financial life to God? Pray. Challenge yourself to commit your financial life fully to God. Write out short phrase that you will say to yourself every time you bring your tithe.

3. Read Genesis 42 and 43, Proverbs 15:22.

a. Compare and contrast the situation of the Egyptians during the drought who followed Joseph's advice and the Israelites who had no plan. What wisdom does this give you as you prepare for your upcoming Jump?

b. Do you have strengths in planning? Be honest. If not, acknowledge this and pray for God to provide someone to help you with this.

4. Based on the above exercises and/or your Daily Devotional readings, write out 1–2 short Spirit Talk phrases that capture God's promises and post them where you can see them regularly.

Coach's Guidance

1. Now that you have committed to fulfilling your Life Mission, how can you "do it more"? It's time to start walking!

   Start by letting other people know what you are interested in doing, so they can help you.

   Identify a place where you can begin to practice fulfilling your mission.

This often starts on a voluntary basis. Depending on your mission, you might simply be able to shift the focus of your daily activities. This is the time to engage and begin the practical learning process.

Each day identify successes when you fulfilled your mission. Keep a running list of these in a journal and share these with your mentors.

2. Depending on your mission, begin to pursue any formal education or certification requirements.

3. Expand your network of people in the area where you will pursue your mission. Start to attend industry events, networking groups, etc. Start to hang around with people doing what you want to do.

4. Plan for success by developing a "Travel Light" plan.

    a. Identify people you need to help you make the plan.

    b. Using the list of what you need to release from the Reflective Exercises, lay out the steps to make the needed changes in your life and begin to move forward.

    c. Create a financial plan that reduces your fixed obligations and increases your reserves. Consult a financial planner to help you or to review your plan.

    d. Talk through your plans with your spouse, mentors and other trusted advisors.

5. Complete the "Overnight Miracle Exercise" described in Step 4, "Visioning."

6. Formalize your Strengths/Character Identity, Life Mission and Vision by writing them all out on a single page. Share this with your mentors. Post it where you can see it regularly.

Move to Exercise 5 after 4–6 weeks.

Step 5 – Exercises
Jump Your Works S!

Reflection Exercises

1. Read Joshua 1 and 3.

    a. Imagine you are Joshua and God is giving you these same instructions. What does God say that gives you confidence to move ahead? God tells Joshua that he will be with him as he was with Moses. Think of the lives of people you know who have journeyed with God. Who is your Moses?

    b. What specific instruction does God give Joshua to ensure that he is successful? What will you put in place to ensure you are committed to follow this instruction? List two people who will hold you accountable and at least two who will be your encouragers.

    c. The Levites carrying the Ark served as guides, because the Israelites had not traveled this path before, yet they too had never followed this path. What is this saying to you in terms of who is guiding your adventure?

    d. What first act of courage was required for God's power to show up? What will be your first act of courage to begin to see God's power displayed? Consider: why might God require us to take this first step?

2. Read Nehemiah 4, Ephesians 6:10–20, John 10:10 and Psalm 35.

    a. What steps did Nehemiah take when was faced with naysayers and enemies opposing what he was doing? How did this affect his commitment to his work? What will you do when you face opposition?

    b. It is said you should know your enemy—remember you are behind enemy lines—who is your opposition? What tactics might he use most effectively against you to derail your mission?

    c. What can you learn from David's prayer regarding dealing with his enemies? How will you armor up to protect yourself?

2. Read Psalm 33 and 127:1–2 and James 4:13–16.

    a. We can be tempted to make plans and focus relentlessly on executing them as we strive to be successful. What do these verses say about how you should approach your mission?

    b. List three character traits you strive to uphold as you venture forth on your mission.

3. Based on the above exercises and/or your Daily Devotional readings, write out 1–2 short Spirit Talk phrases that capture God's promises and post them where you can see them regularly.

Coach's Guidance

1. The rubber hits the road in this step so it is vital to ensure that your Spiritual Disciplines are firmly in place. Review and recommit to your Daily Devotional plan for at least five days/week. Meet with your mentors to affirm that they are prepared to be there for you, directing you toward God, encouraging you and helping talk through attacks from the enemy. Ask them to hold you accountable.

2. Affirm your Life Mission. Post is visibly around where you will see it. Continue to ask yourself each day if what you are doing is "on mission," eliminating things that you are doing that are not. Keep a daily list of "successes," times when you felt you were bearing fruit related to your mission.

3. Gather your strength and courage and make your Jump! Whether that be quitting a job and starting a new one, or setting a new direction for your life's focus.

4. Hold on! Work hard and trust the Lord.

5. Create a running list of testimonials of how God is working in your life. Share with others, glorifying God. Remember that you are contagious when your life is transforming.

6. Make plans celebrate successes regularly with people you love.

Appendix 1

Example List of Character Identities

- Activist
- Advisor
- Advocate
- Analyst
- Architect
- Artist
- Builder
- Coach
- Counselor
- Craftsman
- Creator
- Deal Maker
- Defender
- Designer
- Documenter
- Encourager
- Encyclopedia
- Enforcer
- Entertainer
- Evangelist
- Explorer
- Farmer
- Guardian
- Historian
- Host
- Implementer
- Inventor
- Judge
- Laborer
- Leader
- Maker
- Mediator
- Motivator
- Musician
- Networker
- Nurse
- Nurturer
- Organizer
- Pastor/ Shepherd
- Peacemaker
- Persuader
- Planner
- Preacher
- Problem Solver
- Professor
- Promoter
- Reporter
- Researcher
- Soldier
- Storyteller
- Student
- Teacher
- Team builder
- Technician
- Visionary
- Waiter
- Warrior
- Worshiper
-
-
-
-
-

Appendix 2

Themes

Character Identity   A combination of generically defined roles that describe the essence of a person's core God-given gifting, strengths, and natural abilities. A person will consistently bring this identity to every role he/she plays in life: job, parent, or other. Strive to know your Character Identity and align your life to it more and more.

Vision Killers   People (often those closest to you), ideas, and barriers that prevent you from carrying out your purpose and vision.

Life Mission   The result of applying your Character Identity in the direction of your Obsessive Passions. A concise phrase (seven words or less) that describes what you go out to do all day, every day. Your Life Mission guides your decisions and actions, keeping you on track to fulfill your God-inspired purpose.

Obsessive Passions   Things you just can't seem to stop doing, typically developed in reaction to a past significant hurt or event by applying your strengths to preclude a similar hurt or event. Relentless focus and activity bring relief and, when used to help others, provide a sense of fulfillment and joy.

Spirit Talk	The voice of the Spirit of God—your secret to victory. Post Spirit Talk scriptures and short phrases where you will see them frequently. Read them multiple times a day, allowing the Spirit to reprogram your beliefs.
Jump	The act or releasing old and grasping new, moving you onto the forward slope of the S Curve. On the Works S, releasing an old work and embracing a new one requiring rapid growth. In the case of the Spiritual S, to release an old belief and accept a new belief brings deeper intimacy with God.
Spiritual S	The S Curve that depicts your intimacy with God. In the midst of and following a Jump, intimacy is deep. Over time intimacy fades, giving way to self-reliance. We once again become distanced from God, leaving us begging for a new Jump. Maturation along the Spiritual S leads to oneness with God.
Works S	The S Curve that captures your works: how you use your time. In the midst of and following a Jump, growth—often challenging—is required. Over time, our growth slows, and we begin to stagnate, leading to complacency, boredom, status quo and ultimately obsolescence. Then it is time for a Jump, either self-initiated or due to a forced change. When Jumps on the Works S are inspired by Spiritual S Jumps, the result is movement in the direction of a person's Life Mission.
Surrender	The process of release that occurs on the Spiritual S immediately prior to a Jump. Typically a person will utter the words,

"Lord, I don't want to live my life like this anymore!"

Five-Step Process	The key steps to take to make a meaningful, fulfilling and kingdom impactful Jump on the Works S. The five steps are: Jump Your Spiritual S, Uncover your Character Identity, Align with Mission, Move to Vision and Jump Your Works S!
Travel Light	Preparing for a Works S Jump, inspired by acceptance of God's leadership for the coming Jump, the active elimination of burdens (particularly financial), and development of a plan for the Jump.
Vision	How the world appears after successfully accomplishing your Life Mission.
Emotional Tensions	Seemingly opposite emotions that pull on you at every stage of the S Curves. It is not uncommon to shift from one emotion to an opposing emotion in a matter of seconds.
Locked In	Stranded just past the peak stage of the Works S. Deep-seated fears and lack of vision hold you hostage, keeping you in a place of little growth, growing complacency, and obsolescence.
Old Godly Way	Having come to a fork in the road, you must choose a path. One way seems logical and right from a human point of view; the other, more difficult, requires trust in God. The Old Godly Way is the latter and leads to what you are really seeking.
Dedicated Day	A day (or days) of retreat, alone in a quiet place, accompanied by fasting. This time of extended prayer and reflection should be

filled with scripture reading and journaling. Often pivotal in affirming your Character Identity, Life Mission and direction.

Daily Devotional	A regular, scheduled time to meet with God, read scripture per a reading plan, pray and journal. This provides the scriptural foundation for your Spirit Talk and supports you when you make Jumps.
Team	A select few people (2–4), wise and mature followers of Jesus, who support, encourage, and challenge you. They must be for you and direct you into scripture. It is best to have people of different backgrounds and experiences on your Team. Meet with them every two weeks.
Poking Around	The process of information gathering about different fields that interest you yet know little about. Do this even if you think you understand a field. This is exploratory, not committal. It occurs well in advance of a Works S Jump.

CPSIA information can be obtained
at www.ICGtesting.com
Printed in the USA
FSHW02n0433021018
52538FS